DYNAMICS
OF
RELATIONSHIPS

UNDERSTANDING RELATIONSHIP PROCESSES

Series Editor
Steve Duck, *University of Iowa*

This series of books on the theme **Understanding Relationship Processes** provides a coherent and progressive review of current thinking in the field. Uniquely organized around the notion of relational competence, the six volumes constitute a contemporary, multidisciplinary handbook of relationship research for advanced students and professionals in psychology, sociology, communication, family studies, and education.

Volumes in the Series

1. INDIVIDUALS IN RELATIONSHIPS
2. LEARNING ABOUT RELATIONSHIPS
3. SOCIAL CONTEXT AND RELATIONSHIPS
4. DYNAMICS OF RELATIONSHIPS
5. RELATIONSHIP CHALLENGES
6. UNDERSTUDIED RELATIONSHIPS

EDITED BY
STEVE DUCK

DYNAMICS
OF
RELATIONSHIPS

UNDERSTANDING RELATIONSHIP PROCESSES SERIES
VOLUME 4

SAGE Publications *Rn*
International Educational and Professional Publisher
Thousand Oaks   London   New Delhi

For information address:

SAGE Publications, Inc.
2455 Teller Road
Thousand Oaks, California 91320

SAGE Publications Ltd.
6 Bonhill Street
London EC2A 4PU
United Kingdom

SAGE Publications India Pvt. Ltd.
M-32 Market
Greater Kailash I
New Delhi 110 048 India

Printed in the United States of America

Library of Congress Cataloging-in-Publication Data

Main entry under title:

Dynamics of relationships / edited by Steve Duck.
    p. cm. — (Understanding relationship processes ; v. 4)
   Includes bibliographical references and indexes
   ISBN 0-8039-5413-1. — ISBN 0-8039-5414-X (pbk.)
   1. Interpersonal relations. 2. Man-woman relationships.
  3. Interpersonal communication. I. Duck, Steve. II. Series:
  Understanding relationship processes series; v. 4.
HM132.D95 1994
306.7—dc20   93-48820
                       CIP

94 95 96 97 98 10 9 8 7 6 5 4 3 2 1

Sage Production Editor: Yvonne Könneker

FTW
AGE4319

Contents

Series Preface

This short series of books on a theme, **Understanding Relationship Processes,** responds to recent calls for an attention to process in relationships. A close look at the nature of processes in relationships will reveal that, over and above the importance of change, temporality, and an orientation to the future, there also lies beneath most process thinking on relationships the implicit notion of competent use of knowledge across time. For example, this assumption is true of many elements of the work on relationships, such as the (competent) transition to marriage, (skilled) conflict management, (appropriate) self-disclosure in relationship development, and (orderly) organization or (satisfactory) maintenance of relationships diachronically. The assumption also is contained in any discussion of intimacy assessment or creation of "a couple" (by which authors evaluate the degrees of intimacy or progress that are adequate, allowable, suitable, or competent) and is latent in discussion of relationship breakdown in which discussions treat breakdown as failure or incompetence, contrasted with skill or competence.

Such competence is evident in, and constrained by, a variety of levels of influence on behavior. In focusing on some of these topics, this series moves conceptually outward; that is, the series begins with the contributions of individuals and their developmental experiences to relationships, and moves toward the social context and interpersonal interaction. Individuals bring into relationships their individual characteristics and factors that reflect their point in the life cycle and their developmental achievements. Individuals are influenced by the social setting (situational, cultural, linguistic, and societal) in which the relationship takes place; they are constrained and influenced by the structural, transactional, behavioral, and communicative contexts for their relationships; and they sometimes conduct the relationships in dysfunctional environments or disrupted emotional contexts. The series takes these contextual themes in sequence and deals with the latest research and thinking that address these topics.

Accordingly, each volume focuses on a particular context or arena for relationship activity. The volumes of the series are:

Individuals in Relationships. Volume 1 deals particularly with the ways in which internal or intrapersonal context is provided by structures of the mind or of knowledge that are prerequisite for success in relationships; however, rather than focusing on such things as though they were the end of the story, the chapters place such knowledge styles and structures in context by referring frequently to behavioral effects of such structures.

Learning About Relationships. Volume 2 covers especially the skills and experiences in childhood that lay the groundwork for competence as a properly functioning relater in adult life; the volume emphasizes the wide range of social sources from which development of competence is derived and the richness of the social sources from which developing minds acquire their sense of relationship competence.

Social Context and Relationships. Volume 3 focuses especially on the social structural constraints within which relationships are located and the ways in which the two partners must negotiate and deal with the dialectical and interior pressures created by such contexts.

Dynamics of Relationships. Volume 4 deals with the dyadic management of relational conduct in the context provided by the earlier volumes, and explores the issues of competent relational management that are created by the transactions of relating—not the factors that influence or prepare the ground for relationships, but the actual doing of them.

Relationship Challenges (S. Duck & J. T. Wood, coeditors). Volume 5 turns the series toward the difficult side of relationships and away from any implication that relationships are only good and delightful. Relationship processes encompass "binds" as well as "bonds" (in Wiseman's 1986 elegant pun), and these binds must be included in an understanding of relationship processes.

Understudied Relationships: Off the Beaten Track (J. T. Wood & S. Duck, coeditors). Volume 6 is based on the fact that recent scholarly study of relationships (a) has been overbalanced toward particular types of relationship and (b) tends to overlook types that occur frequently in the real world. A full understanding of relationship processes must include consideration of theoretically inconvenient instances as well as others.

STEVE DUCK

Volume Preface

The first two volumes in this series, **Understanding Relationship Processes**, outline the contribution of individual knowledge to the conduct of relationships, whether from the point of view of cognitive structure or of the learning that takes place in childhood. The next two volumes explore the relational contexts provided respectively by various external, nonindividual, and nondyadic influences, and by interior, dynamic, transactional processes. Volume 3 (*Social Context and Relationships*) focused on contexts provided by various social, cultural, structural, and network processes. Now Volume 4 focuses on the sense in which specific relational behaviors are located in sequences and in partners' continual accommodations to one another.

The first three volumes thus cover important issues that set the scene for consideration of the transactional dynamics of relationships in this sense. Much background is inferred, much history assumed, and much cultural knowledge "understood" in the competent conduct of relationships. However, also necessary to successful relationship transactions are several essentially dyadic skills, such as the management of conversation, the development and practical use of relational knowledge, the ability to listen to others, the ability to manage the here-and-now sequencing of nonverbal behavior and talk, the development of dispositional beliefs about partner, and an awareness of the future as a shaper of the relationship. Such dispositional beliefs, such as enduring trust, reflect the extensions and expectations made by partners on the basis of past experience. The present volume thus deals with the here-and-now dyadic management of relational conduct in the contexts provided by the earlier volumes while yet emphasizing that such processes are based in expectations about the future. The whole process is summarized in the volume's title, *Dynamics of Relationships.*

This volume further indicates the effects of not only the past but also the expectations that are the pipers at the gates of the future of any relationship. It is natural for researchers to focus on the past and the history of relationships as guides to explanation, just as it is natural for human beings to use the past as a guide to everything that they expect to see unfold. However, as I have argued at greater length elsewhere (Duck, 1990, 1994a, 1994b), relationships are driven by a need to create meaning as a way to cope with the uncertainties of an unfolding future that places yesterday in a sequence of other days. The present volume therefore (sometimes implicitly) looks at the context provided by the fact that relationships occur in a context of "ongoingness" (Bennett, in press), built on a real past and an extended future that each exert an influence on the meaning of relational behavior in the present (Duck, 1994b).

This volume and the series thus challenge the appearance in much research that relationships consist of single interactions devoid of contexts, or are based on the short-term interactions most often used as the basis of laboratory work on close relationships. Generalizations derived from such reduced situations extracted from the dynamics of everyday life are increasingly condemned as risking vacuity. This volume attempts to help to theorize relational dynamics as processes in this sense and to demonstrate some of the ways in which relationships are more than mere sequences of behavior or cumulations of individual acts but gain their existence from the meanings of such sequences and cumulations. It is the investment of such things with dynamic continuity that provides a context for partners to comprehend their connectedness to one another.

The first chapter, by Sally Planalp and Kathy Garvin-Doxas, neatly illustrates the above points by taking a concept that has had great currency in relationships research, namely relationship knowledge, and, instead of treating it as a purely individual property, exploring the effects that it creates in the dynamics of conversation. As the authors note, the acts of acquiring, using, and maintaining mutual knowledge create an ongoing process—a process that becomes increasingly sophisticated and complex the better we know someone, and that goes on virtually constantly. This emphasis is especially important in relation to a topic (relational knowledge) that typically has been seen in static terms or as based on mere accumulation of information, with little attention paid to the transformative effects of new information as it develops a perceiver's understanding. Equally the authors strike the important, if muted, note that serves as counterpoint to much of the present series: a demonstration of the value of a truly interdisciplinary approach to relationship study. The authors suggest that:

> linguists tend to look at how mutual knowledge is used in conversation. Communication scholars tend to look at what is achieved or is not achieved (often socially) through the use or misuse of mutual knowledge. Psychologists tend to focus on the acquisition and use of knowledge without worrying about its mutuality; social psychologists tend to focus on its mutuality or its use in social contexts. Sociologists may consider how intersubjectivity is achieved; philosophers may consider whether true intersubjectivity is possible.

Chapter 2, by Kathryn Dindia, illustrates these points another way in the context of discussing one of the classic topics of relationship research: self-disclosure. Dindia notes that for too long self-disclosure has been treated merely as an act. She points out that self-disclosure is better conceived as a dynamic relational process, and that processes are always more complicated than acts. In reviewing three perspectives on self-disclosure (self-disclosure viewed as an act, as an interpersonal process, and as an intrapersonal process), Dindia argues that self-disclosure requires considerably more knowledge and skill than is implied by the simple act perspective. By weaving together the interpersonal and intrapersonal processes of self-disclosure Dindia is able to show how self-disclosure is a dynamic and open-ended process that constructs both persons and relationships, both in the long term (for example, in respect to relational development and maintenance) and in the short term (in respect to the specific interactional dynamics of relationship episodes).

Ted Spencer's chapter follows with a development of this theme in other ways by demonstrating in detail how the interactional and dynamic management of talk serves the function of regulating both individual identity and relationships between family members. Spencer proposes a cogent critique of previous research based on four ways in which it has underestimated the role of ordinary talk in transforming individual identity and relationship dynamics: (a) an impoverished model of talk as though it served merely as a clear-channel conduit for the transmission and receipt of unambiguous information, (b) a narrow attention only to crises or to special-purpose talk, (c) a tendency to strip individual utterances away from the larger conversational sequences in which they are situated, and (d) a failure to examine the long-term and short-term relational goals that are enacted by specific key features of talk.

Drawing on a consideration of such long-term goals of relationships, Susan D. Boon (Chapter 4) considers the role of risk and vulnerability within the broader context of relationship phenomena that are both light and dark. Boon focuses on the ways in which partners negotiate the dilemmas they face as their relationship progresses and the partners shape the nature of the bonds between them. The chapter stresses the role of the present and past actions of partners in the long-term context of relationship dynamics and partners' continual juxtaposition of the dark and light elements in any relationship. Boon depicts the development of trust as a long-term negotiation involving risk and a symbolic meaning that transcends the specifics of individual moment-by-moment transactions.

In like manner, Michael Monsour's chapter focuses on the long-term cognitive and interactional competencies involved in communicating knowledge about oneself during the course of an interaction. His chapter analyzes the management, acquisition, and organization of knowledge about one's relational partner into a coherent and at least partially shared relational whole, through ordinary communication about similarity and dissimilarity. The chapter reviews the similarity construct and expands it to show that competent communication and comprehension of dis/similarities result in the sharing of meaning between relational partners. He argues that long-term creation of mutual understanding of similarities and differences between relational partners facilitates a shared perceptual reality, a reality that may encourage or deter the pursuit of intimacy in the relationship. As implied above, Monsour's chapter views similarity as an extended social process rather than as a cognitive state existing between two minds. The construction of meaning is instrumental in building the quality of relationship created by the two partners together.

The final chapter, by Maureen P. Keeley and Allen J. Hart, considers the same issue of quality but relates it to the important behavioral underpinnings that are too easily forgotten in research on relationships, namely the coordination of nonverbal behavior. Clearly much understanding, much trust, most disclosure, and much acquisition of knowledge are enacted in the dynamic behaviors of interactions, many of them nonverbal. Nonverbal communication is inherently dynamic and conveys relational messages of considerable power that, by their very ephemeral nature, can register changes in feelings or consolidation of affection in ways that words sometimes lag behind. The chapter thus rounds out a consideration of some of the elements of meaning and relational dynamics that together render relationships as complex as they are to understand.

Together the chapters in the present volume add considerable depth of perspective to understanding relationship processes by indicating the dynamic crucible in which amalgamation of all the interior and exterior influences takes place. They thus follow up on the argument implicit in the third volume of the series: that relationships have to be enacted and are practical things with practical implications, not merely outcomes produced by cognitive states or relational history. Relationships are constructed and forged by real human beings facing everyday dilemmas and dynamically wrestling to construct a meaningful interpretation of life's continually changing contingencies.

STEVE DUCK

1

Using Mutual Knowledge in Conversation: Friends as Experts on Each Other

Sally Planalp

Kathy Garvin-Doxas

Alex goes to his good friend Barb's party, where he meets another friend of Barb's named Cory. Alex and Cory talk about how nice Barb is, the latest political controversy, and the weather. While discussing the weather, they find out that they both windsurf, so they spend another hour talking about technique, equipment, and places to go.

Later, Alex gets a chance to talk to Barb. She asks him how his plans for a skiing vacation are shaping up and what his mother had to say when she called back. He asks her what time her interview is on Monday and whether she's as anxious as she was during her last one.

Meanwhile, Cory has run into his ex-roommate David. He notices that David still drinks a lot and wonders whether he ever got his driver's license back, but he doesn't really care because he considers their friendship over.

1

These examples illustrate how pervasive and important mutual knowledge is for people who are just getting acquainted, for people who know each other well, and even for people who would rather they did not know each other. By mutual knowledge, we mean the knowledge that two people share, know they share, and use in interacting with one another. Alex and Cory both know they know Barb because she introduced them. They both know about windsurfing, but did not know they knew until it came up in conversation. Alex and Barb know a great deal about one another—plans, past events such as phone calls and job interviews, how the other is likely to be feeling—and they take this knowledge for granted in their conversations. Cory still knows about his ex-roommate's habits but he does not know about David's current life and does not care to find out.

The process of using mutual knowledge in conversation ties in closely to the themes that have guided this six-volume series and this volume in particular. First, acquiring and using mutual knowledge are integral to being socially competent. If you use mutual knowledge well, you can be an interesting conversational partner and an understanding friend; if you use it poorly, you can create misunderstandings and offend people. Being competent requires learning about an infinite range of topics, learning what a large number of other people know about those topics, remembering and accessing that knowledge when needed, making reasonable guesses when you are not sure, presuming it (or not presuming it) when producing your own messages and when interpreting others' messages, and keeping up to date all the time. The skill involved is formidable.

Second, the sequence of acquiring, using, and maintaining mutual knowledge is an ongoing process. It begins before we meet someone (when we acquire the knowledge that we will use later in conversations) and it goes on through every conversation we have with that person. It may become the basis for mutual understanding and closeness. It often continues even when we are away from each other and after we have lost contact. The process becomes increasingly sophisticated and complex the better we know someone, and it goes on virtually constantly.

Third, the study of mutual knowledge, its development and its use, is widely multidisciplinary. To get a full picture of how mutual knowledge works you must look at work in linguistics (Smith, 1982), communication (Nofsinger, 1989), cognitive psychology (Ericsson & Smith, 1991), social psychology (Wegner, 1987), philosophy (Schutz, 1967), and sociology (Schegloff, 1992). The emphases are different but the subject matter is essentially the same. For instance, linguists tend to look at how mutual knowledge is used in conversation. Communication scholars tend to look at what is or is not achieved (often socially) through the use or misuse of mutual knowledge. Psychologists tend to focus on the acquisition and use of knowledge without worrying about its mutuality; social psychologists tend to focus on its mutuality or on its use in social contexts. Sociologists may consider how intersubjectivity is achieved; philosophers may consider whether true intersubjectivity is possible.

Finally, there are many connections between our chapter and other chapters in this volume and in other volumes of this series, but there are also some differences. Several of the chapters in Volume 1 deal with the use of knowledge much as we do, but their focus is on individuals' knowledge, whereas ours is on the knowledge that individuals share. The contributors of Volume 1 tend to emphasize how individuals conceive of and process information about relationships, whereas we tend to emphasize how relational processes are founded in all types of knowledge that individuals have. Put more concretely, they tend to look at how Alex and Barb conceive of each other and their relationship and how they process relevant information. We look at how

Alex's and Barb's mutual knowledge about anything—Guatemalan textiles, what they did last weekend, the national debt, or an upcoming job interview—influences how they interact and relate with one another.

Volume 2 centers on developmental processes, of which the acquisition, use, and decay of mutual knowledge is certainly one. Volume 2 traces development across the life span, whereas our chapter traces development across relationships only for adults. Just noting the comparison, however, does raise the issue of whether the process of acquiring knowledge is much the same for children and adults. Children are, after all, "universal novices" whereas adults are novices in only some things (if only adults were "universal experts"!).

Volume 3 contains chapters on the social context of relationships, including third-party influences on relationships, the influence of daily routines, and social networks. Our chapter relates to each of these. For example, acquaintances and friends talk a lot about third parties, drawing on varying degrees of mutual knowledge to talk about them (what we pejoratively call gossip). Daily routines are another important topic, especially for friends who often know each other's daily schedules, habits, and plans. Finally, social networks make using mutual knowledge enormously difficult. Just talking with two friends at the same time requires keeping track of what each knows and does not know. Keeping mutual knowledge up-to-date with a large number of people is a big challenge, as we all realize when we forget to tell someone that the party was called off or when we ask about how someone is doing when that person died years ago. Anyone who has escaped from a dense network also appreciates how refreshing it is not to have to keep track of what you are and are not supposed to know, to tell your own version of a story, or to meet someone who does not know all about you already.

Volume 5 considers topics such as reconfigured families, long-distance relationships, and enemies. These provoke questions related to mutual knowledge as well. Do new members of reconfigured families feel left out of discussions that require extensive mutual knowledge, such as knowing about Aunt Betty's kleptomania or the city some family members used to live in? Are partners in long-distance relationships able to keep up on each others' lives by phone or mail, or do they give up and live for the moment? And finally, what kind of strange intimacy comes from knowing all about and yet hating someone?

The theme of Volume 6 is understudied relationships, including the relationships of gays and lesbians, members of ethnic minorities, and partners from different generations, as well as relationships that have developed overnight, over decades, or over E-mail. We can only speculate about connections with our own work here. Perhaps gays, lesbians, African Americans, Latinos/ Latinas, and the elderly find it especially difficult to find common ground with others but especially rewarding when they do. We also might ask what kind of shortcuts people use to develop mutual knowledge in "instant intimacy," what special intimacy comes from knowing someone most of your life, and how mutual knowledge develops differently when it is based entirely on interaction over E-mail instead of on face-to-face interaction.

Now that we know (and we know that we know) how mutual knowledge links up with many important themes, issues, and topics covered in this series, let us consider how mutual knowledge works in conversation.

Mutual Knowledge in (Inter)Action

Unlike other cognitive processes that underlie interaction and relationships, the use of mutual knowledge is clearly visible to the naked eye (or more likely, ear). When naive observers were asked to listen to taped conversations and to decide whether they were between friends or between acquaintances, mutual knowledge (or the lack thereof) was cited more often than any other reason for believing people were friends or believing they were acquaintances (Planalp & Benson, 1992). When judgments of trained coders were used as input into statistical discriminations between friends' and acquaintances' conversation, mutual knowledge was the most powerful of 24 variables, including intimacy of self-disclosure, formality, spontaneity, and references to past, present, and future (Planalp, 1993). In other words, friends talk in ways that reflect certain kinds of mutual knowledge, acquaintances talk in ways that reflect their lack of knowledge, and this difference is apparent to almost anyone who listens.

To illustrate, here are excerpts from two conversations, one between friends and the other between acquaintances. These and all excerpts in this chapter come from conversations between college students speaking on topics of their own choosing, audiotaped and transcribed by the students themselves, with transcripts refined by Planalp based on the audiotapes.

Conversation Segment 1

Person A: My roommate's name is Tad. I always kid him, man. Like it's a big thing on campus. . . . Well, I'm not in any fraternity or anything, but a lot of my friends are Sigma Chi's, what have you. And, like, they all changed their name. For instance, Saul, my roommate, decides to call himself Tad, I'm like . . .

Person B: His name is Saul?

Person A: His name is Saul, but you call him Tad.

Conversation Segment 2

Person C: I've got all the tables and stuff worked out. Brad's stressing on it. He came by about 20 minutes ago. "Are we supposed to make a graph or a table for this one?" I'm like, "I don't know, man." Cause she's in class today, "I want graphs and tables and all these summaries and stuff," and I'm just going, "Oh, man." So . . .

Person D: You might be able to rig up something on Kev's computer.

The difference between these conversations in terms of mutual knowledge should be obvious. Person A assumes that Person B does not know things that friends ought to know about one another: that his roommate's name is Tad (changed from Saul) and that he is not in a fraternity. Acquaintances have to explain these things. Person C, on the other hand, assumes that Person D knows who Brad is and Person D assumes that Person C knows who Kev is and that he has a computer. Friends tend to know each other's friends, or at least know about them. These kinds of examples are commonplace in conversation.

How People Use Mutual Knowledge in Conversation

Research on conversational processes shows that mutual knowledge is absolutely fundamental to communication (Clark, 1992; Isaacs & Clark, 1987). Listeners understand messages by drawing on vast stores of existing knowledge and by adding new information that is gleaned from messages. Speakers design their messages taking into account what listeners already know and what is new in their messages (Clark & Schaefer, 1989; Grice, 1975; Wilkes-Gibbs & Clark, 1992). Clark's pioneering research on the given-new contract (Clark & Haviland, 1977) demonstrates this process at the most basic level—the level of the sentence. Competent communicators accent new information so listeners can separate it from what they already know and add it to their store of knowledge (at least temporarily). For example, if you had brought in several pieces of fruit for lunch, I might say, "I want that *apple.*" I assume you know that I want a piece of fruit; the question is which one. On the other hand, if you were cleaning out the refrigerator and started to throw away an apple, I might say, "I *want* that apple." I assume you know about the apple; what you do not know is that I want it.

Mutual knowledge helps listeners and speakers perform other important tasks in conversations as well. For example, listeners use mutual knowledge to make conversations coherent, to ask and answer questions appropriately, to derive the gist of a message, to draw out important inferences, and to remember important points (Chiesi, Spilich, & Voss, 1979; Smith, 1982; Spilich, Vesonder, Chiesi, & Voss, 1979). In this way, new information is continuously added to old information in a coherent building process that eventually creates the huge edifices of knowledge that we all have and use to communicate.

Although everyone uses mutual knowledge continuously in conversation, strangers, acquaintances, and friends draw their mutual knowledge from different sources. Strangers draw primarily on knowledge based on *community membership* (Clark & Marshall, 1981) or knowledge that we have because we are *contemporaries* (Schutz, 1967), living at roughly the same time in roughly the same place. For example, we can assume that most strangers know what the weather is like, who is president of the United States, and what direction is north. Typical conversational openers commenting on the weather, sports, or some salient public event demonstrate strangers' reliance on this knowledge to get conversations started. Strangers also engage in *setting talk* (Maynard & Zimmerman, 1984). For example, if you meet someone at an art museum, you may strike up a conversation about the museum or about art.

Two other sources of mutual knowledge are *physical copresence* (being together) and *linguistic copresence* (talking together) (Clark & Marshall, 1981), or knowledge that we have because we are *consociates* (Schutz, 1967). These sources are available to acquaintances in very limited ways because of their limited experience together and to friends to a much greater extent, depending on how much they have been together and/or talked. For instance, one acquaintance drew on very limited physical copresence when she said:

Person A: I was so lucky you were at Bennigan's that night.

These friends relied on linguistic copresence when they referred to a previous conversation:

Person A: So what did Bart want last night?
Person B: Well, I told you, he's coming out to Colorado.

Different sources of mutual knowledge may make a qualitative difference in the type of relationship that emerges. For example, you may hire a private investigator to uncover information about a friend's activities and interests, but that same information has a different quality when it is offered freely in a pleasant conversation. Several more factors are at work in conversation, including opportunities to explore issues in greater depth, to learn more about what the information means to the partner, to develop trust, to reciprocate, and to explore issues together. Similarly, you may hear all about your friend's trip to Italy, but it is not the same as going with her. Or you may go with her, but your shared knowledge has a different quality if you never talk about what you have experienced together. Even though you both saw the Pietà and ate lasagna, your experience may be enhanced by her knowledge of Michelangelo's work and her experience may be enhanced by your knowledge of Tuscan cuisine. She may have noticed where the Pietà was repaired when you did not, and you may have noticed what herbs were used in the lasagna when she did not.

One of the problems of mutual knowledge, then, is that we never really know for sure that another person knows something. You may have gone to a movie with someone, so you assume that she can talk about the movie, but she may have been asleep, distracted, or just did not get it. You may have told Y about a concert in an earlier conversation, but you may forget that you told him and tell him again. We may assume college students know about Plato when they do not; we may assume someone we just met does not know our next-door neighbor when she does. These failures become apparent in conversation when someone attempts a repair (Maynard & Zimmerman, 1984; Nofsinger, 1989; Schegloff, 1992). For example, here is a failure of community-based knowledge:

Person A: . . . you go from NCAR over a little bit.
Person B: Where is NCAR, anyway?

For those not in the know, NCAR refers to the National Center for Atmospheric Research in Boulder, Colorado. If you have never been to Boulder or you are not a meteorologist, you probably did not know that either.

Even when errors are not apparent, conversational partners assess each other's mutual knowledge as an ongoing part of conversation (Isaacs & Clark, 1987). If a person knows something, she may let her partner know to save further explanation, as in the following segment:

Person A: I just transferred up here this semester, from, um . . . Front Range, down in Westminster.
Person B: Yeah, I know some people who go down there.

People also assess their partners' mutual knowledge by whether they ask questions, whether they make comments that are relevant, and whether they are able to make appropriate inferences. For example, friends are able to draw inferences about their partners' personal relationships:

Person A: I don't think he is very used to relationships at all. You know? That was like, I mean, I think you were one of the biggest relationships he's ever had.
Person B: Well, I don't know. Some of the people he's dated were kind of Cheez-Whiz, too, so . . .
Person A: And it totally threw him that you weren't.
Person B: Trying not to be, anyway. I don't know, he was just . . . that was a really weird situation.

We suspect that the filler "y'know?" or "you know?" (also used in the example above) is a way of checking mutual knowledge and often is used unconsciously at change points in conversation to make sure the partner is following a new train of thought (Goldberg, 1983).

How Acquaintances Use Mutual Knowledge

A great deal of conversation in beginning relationships is devoted to searching for and developing mutual knowledge so partners can carry on an interesting conversation and have the basis for more talk in the future (Kent, Davis, & Shapiro, 1981).

These two people, for instance, discovered immediately that they had something in common.

Person A: Um. So, where are you from?

Person B: Uh, I'm from Pueblo.

Person A: I'm from Pueblo, too! Were you, where'd you go to school?

Person B: I went to Pueblo County.

Person A: I went to South.

In the conversations between college students that we taped, partners often talked about people they might know in common (especially through sororities and fraternities), their hometowns, their classes, and various activities such as tennis or concerts. Sometimes conversational partners talked about someone they both might know, but explored other topics as they came up, as is illustrated in the following segment:

Person A: Yeah, um . . . we went, we like, um, walked by the Sink on Thursday night and I saw Andy, Andy . . . pledge Andy.

Person B: Andy?

A: I don't really know all of them yet.

B: I don't know.

A: Oh, and, um, John Padilla was with them for a little.

B: Oh really?

A: Yeah. He was sitting outside.

B: Yeah.

A: Yeah. So I was talking to them for a little.

B: That's cool.

A: Yeah.

B: I mean, do you know Andy's last name?

A: Um.

B: Is it . . . Is it Andy Moore?

A: I don't know. Is . . .

B: Like tall, brown hair?

A: It blond?

B: Oh, blond.

A: Well, kind . . . well, I'm not sure.

B: Does he live in the house?

A: No. He lives somewhere like on Baseline. He's a pledge.

B: 'Cause I know there's an Andy that lives in the house. Andy Moore.

A: I know Andy Clarke. (laugh)

B: Andy Clarke, yeah. He's not a pledge though.

A: No.

B: Actually, we call them associate members.

A: Yeah, but that's Darrell, like, yeah.

B: Yeah.

A: But it's easier just to call them pledges because that's what everyone else knows them as anyway.

B: I know.

A: You're like, what's an associate member?

B: (laugh)

A: Gee, I don't know.

B: It's just a nicer word for pledge.

A: Yeah, it's just 'cause, you know, we don't haze.

B: Yeah, though, that's good. Yeah. But . . . um . . . last year. I lived in Baker with Darrell and Chris Johnson and Tom.

A: Oh really?

B: Yeah. And Tom and Chris had a room that connected to Andy and they were always in there playing Nintendo and stuff (laugh) but I don't know his last name, but . . .

A: It's the Sega generation now.

B: Oh, okay, whatever. I don't do it [laugh]. But whenever I come over here, I always dance with him, so maybe I should ask him his last name.

A: [laugh]

B: [laugh]

A: Just so you can tell other people. [laugh]

B: Yeah. [laugh]

Even though these two people never met before this conversation, it is clear that they both know John Padilla, Andy Clarke, Darrell, Chris Johnson, and Tom and that they may or may not know the same Andy What's-His-Name (Moore?).

In addition to discovering mutual knowledge, acquaintances exchanged biographical information. It is apparent that new acquaintances know nothing about each other:

Person A: Oh. What do you do?

Person B: I'm, uh, an O.R. tech, which is the equivalent to scrub nurse in civilian life.

Person A: Wow.

Person B: I assist doctors in operations and stuff like that.

In the conversations we taped, partners seldom pursued a simple name/rank/serial number strategy. More often they would ask questions such as "where are you from" and "what's your major" but would go into a topic in greater depth if they found that they both knew a lot about it. When they did find these integrating topics, the level of intimacy might be much higher for those topics than for the ones that were mentioned and dropped.

This raises the question of whether this type of talk in early interactions constitutes self-disclosure or just searching for something to talk about. To a certain extent it is both, in that we can always tell the other person about ourselves without running out of things to say. But this is probably neither typical nor particularly socially adept. Lonely, boring people talk about themselves (Jones, Hobbs, & Hockenbury, 1982; Leary, Rogers, Canfield, & Coe, 1986). It is better to let partners have turns talking about themselves, but even better to find things that both people can talk about together. This is what most of the college students we taped did: They tried to find out what they had in common or talked about things they assumed that they had in common. They did not seem to be particularly interested in revealing themselves or in finding out about their partners. The conversation cited above about the O.R. technician is not a typical case; the one about Andy What's-His-Name is.

There are, of course, circumstances that may make self-disclosure more likely. For example, if two people are put in a room to be videotaped and are asked to talk, they may talk about themselves for lack of anything else. If they had met at a conference, for instance, they might talk about the conference papers. If two people are testing the waters for a long-term relationship—first dates or first meetings between roommates, for instance—they may talk about each other because such information will be needed down the road anyway. But many people carry on brief, sometimes interesting, conversations and never see each other again. Their talk is founded on mutual knowledge, not self-disclosure.

Of the many topics that people have in common, however, some are more appropriate than others in certain settings or in certain relationships. One could talk about weather and about art in an art museum, but art is perhaps more interesting, shows more sensitivity to the other's interests, and may lead to further conversation. We can all discover a degree of mutual knowledge about sex, personal problems, and highly loaded issues in politics and religion, but we ordinarily save those topics for later in a relationship. We may not talk about sex or our personal problems with coworkers because it simply is not done (following norms of self-disclosure) or because the information is irrelevant for the tasks that we do together. We may not discuss loaded issues with people we do not know well, not for fear of being judged badly, but for fear of being misunderstood if the proper groundwork in mutual knowledge is not laid in advance.

Regardless of whether the goal is to have a pleasant conversation or to learn about each other, skilled interactors also have meta-knowledge about social interaction, or knowledge about how to acquire knowledge. They know the appropriate scripts or social routines for asking questions in ways that express curiosity but not intrusiveness (Berger & Kellermann, 1983; Douglas, 1984). For example, when comparing experiences to write this chapter, we realized that we are both less skilled than others we know. Garvin-Doxas was struck by how skillfully one of her colleagues asked a prospective graduate student about herself. Planalp grew up in a very small town where everyone knew everyone else and was not confronted with the task of acquiring information about other people from scratch until she went to college. She still feels she is being intrusive when asking any kind of personal question, even though she just wrote the section of this chapter on such questions being appropriate and necessary.

How Friends Use Mutual Knowledge

Friends use mutual knowledge very differently than acquaintances do. Friends covered name, rank, and serial-number information long ago; instead, they assume knowledge of each other's lives, especially their present lives, and use it almost constantly in conversation (Kent et al., 1981). Here are some examples:

Person A: You're like, ah . . . pinned.
Person B: And then I really can't see Rob pinning me at all. I would laugh. I mean he's just not that romantic type of guy so I don't, I mean, could you see him pinning me?
Person A: That's a scream.
Person B: No. I mean I can't see him that committed to anybody, you know? It's just weird.

Clearly, B knows that A knows a fair amount about her boyfriend, Rob, and how likely he is to make a commitment to her or anybody else. She takes it for granted in her rhetorical question. Friends also know about specific events in each other's lives:

Person A: Uh, tell me about your party last night, then.

about each other's plans and schedules:

Person A: But, uh . . . so you're thinking of living in the Cape this summer, huh?
Person B: Yes, yes, yes, yes.

and about each other's habits:

Person A: I guess so. Well, you never get your work done when I'm gone. . . . You just loaf around . . . .

Person B: What do you mean I don't get my work done? I got a shitload done last weekend.

Person A: At the last minute!

One of the essential tasks of friendship seems to be keeping up-to-date on each other's lives. And, as a friend of the first author pointed out after reading a draft of this manuscript, sharing lives—living someone else's life as well as your own—is one of the great joys of friendship, something we fall to immediately after long absences. This may be why Duck, Rutt, Hurst, and Strejc (1991) found that the mere occurrences of conversations (even though they were full of acknowledged trivial information) were rated as "highly important" by respondents. As the examples illustrate, the conversations we analyzed were full of updates on classwork, a party the night before, what the landlord said, yesterday's bike ride, what's going on at work, and so on. In one particularly interesting case, the speaker used conversation with a friend to keep up-to-date on his own life.

Person A: I didn't drink at all yesterday, did I?

Person B: Yeah, you did. You and Rob had a pitcher of beer.

Person A: Oh, yeah.

Other people are an especially common topic. Here is one example:

Person A: Tobey's moving out with her man, did I tell you?

Person B: Hmm huh

Person A: St. Louis . . . she's gonna be rich, he's . . . I think he's a babe.

Person B: When is she moving?

In an earlier study (Planalp, 1993), evidence for the presence or absence of mutual knowledge was coded in 36 conversations. Six general types of knowledge were found: knowledge of (a) other people, (b) biographical information, (c) the partner's present life, (d) a particular event, (e) the partner's schedule and plans, and (f) the partner's habits (as illustrated above). The types that discriminated best were friends' mutual knowledge of other people ($p < .000$), friends' knowledge of the partner's present life ($p < .002$), friends' knowledge of a particular event ($p < .003$), and acquaintances' lack of knowledge of biographical information ($p < .092$).

Friends obviously know a lot about one another, but they are not above making errors. They may, for example, be in the same place at the same time and not realize it:

Person A: Oh, my Lord, they had this guy out in front of the UMC talking . . .

Person B: Noah, I was there!

Person A: Oh, Lord. Oh, I think that's why I have this migraine because I was just so . . .

Person B: Me, too.

Person A: I, I was so upset.

Person B: He was such an asshole.

Or one person may think the other knows something that he does not:

Person A: I have a little point to make. Your little white friend got off with the cops, but what about the black guy at the party who got arrested . . .

Person B: What black guy?

Person A: You didn't know? I didn't tell you this?

Person B: What, at the party Friday night?

Person A: Yeah.

Person B: No.

Friends also continue to discover new things about each other as they come up in conversation later in their relationships:

Person A: I was going out with Billy.
Person B: So?
A: Well, I was going out with him the first month I got to school.
B: Liar.
A: What do you mean, "liar"?
B: It's easy to make up stories two years after.
A: Ask anyone. I started going out with Billy in September.
B: Sure you did.
A: In September.
B: And where is this alleged Billy now?
A: He's in New Orleans.
B: Of course he is.
A: Wanna see pictures? I'm gonna show you fucking pictures of this guy.
B: Sure, like this couldn't be your cousin or something.
A: No! It's not my cousin.

Considering the enormous amount of knowledge that each person brings to bear when talking to a friend, the question arises of how we are able to talk to more than one person at a time. Although this process is not well understood, it may be akin to code-switching (Clark & Marshall, 1981), such as when we speak Spanish with one friend and English with another. We access the right knowledge (in this case, knowledge of the language) when needed. That does not, however, solve the problem of having to talk with an acquaintance and a friend at the same time. We can use our mutual knowledge with the friend and leave the acquaintance out of much of what is going on; we can set aside our mutual knowledge and give explanations that the friend does not need; or we can make some foul compromise between the two. This may be one problem of social life that simply has no good solution.

If we have large social networks, we also are confronted with the nearly overwhelming task of keeping up-to-date with many people (another version of "keeping up with the Joneses"). I am expected to remember, for example, term-paper topics for 120 students, when Eric is coming to visit, how Renee's sister is doing, when Jürgen is leaving for Germany, how Genie is getting along with Randy, and what conference Kristine just attended. If I am ever sworn to secrecy, I also must remember what I am *not* supposed to know about various people or various events. It is no wonder that there are so many belated-birthday cards in shops, that salespeople have Rolodexes with the names of clients' spouses and children, and that many confidences are broken unawares.

How are we able to remember all this and keep adding to our store of information as we develop long-term relationships with people whose lives are changing constantly? Current research on expertise (e.g., Chi, Glaser, & Farr, 1988; Ericsson & Smith, 1991) indicates that experts (compared to novices) are able to "chunk" or organize knowledge in meaningful ways and to perceive complex patterns in incoming information. In other words, experts do not remember huge quantities of isolated details; they remember complex and interrelated patterns. As a consequence, experts know more and they are able to learn faster than novices (Scardamalia & Bereiter, 1991). With knowledge, as with money, the rich get richer. The poor do not get poorer, but they do not get rich as fast.

Friends are, in essence, experts on one another and they seem to reap many of the advantages that experts show in other domains. For example, they are more efficient in their talk. They know what words their partners will understand so they do not have to give elaborate descriptions (Isaacs & Clark, 1987; Wilkes-Gibbs & Clark, 1992). Friends refer frequently to types of people ("granolas," "geeks," "hotties"), places (The Sink, Tulagi's), pop culture (The Samples), and important events (next year when someone turns 21). We found no evidence of friends using expressions that are unique to the dyad (called "private keys" or "idiomatic expressions"), although others have (Bell & Healey, 1992; Clark & Schaefer, 1987).

If people share mutual knowledge, they also are saved the trouble of checking assumptions or filling in additional information when they talk. For instance, compare these two segments of one person talking with a friend and the same person talking about basically the same information with an acquaintance:

Conversation With Friend

Person A: So, what about The Samples on Saturday night?

Person B: Umm, I want to go and I haven't bought a ticket and they're not sold out or anything, but . . .

Conversation With Acquaintance

Person A: I don't, we're, um, have you, do you listen to The Samples at all?

Person B: Oh.

Person A: They're a reggae band. They're going to Red Rocks on Saturday.

Person B: Red Rocks.

Person A: Uh-huh.

Person B: Yeah.

Clearly the friends have talked about the concert before, so they can get down to the key question right away—are you going? With the acquaintance, Person A seems to hesitate about how to talk about the concert and realizes that she first needs to ask Person B whether the latter knows who The Samples are before she can say more about them. Acquaintances also may ask for additional information that is needed to understand, as in these parallel conversations, again, between one person and two different partners.

Conversation With Friend

Person A: . . . And, I went to work. It's just been like the longest day though, you know. It's just dragging like on and on. I had four customers tonight at work.

Person B: Uh, um, uh-huh.

Person A: Four, I was just like, I was so bored. I was talking on the phone, Sasha wasn't working though, so I couldn't talk to her. I was just like, it was just awful. So boring.

Conversation With Acquaintance

Person A: Yeah, it's a pretty neat store. It's just really slow and boring. I only had like four customers in tonight.

Person B: That's cool. Do you have time to like do your homework and study for tests and stuff, then?

Person A: Yeah, I do, but I usually talk on the phone the whole time.

In the first conversation, she tells her friend about her day being boring and mentions that she could not talk to Sasha. The acquaintance, however, asks her what she does when work is boring and she has to explain that she usually talks on the phone, not even mentioning that she usually talks with Sasha but could not yesterday. Presumably the friend already knows everything the acquaintance had to ask and presumably the acquaintance did not care about whether she talked to Sasha or not.

Experts also have a deeper understanding of the domain in which they are experts. If friends are like other experts, they are able to go back and forth in sophisticated ways between what they are learning and what they already knew, using new information to update existing knowledge and using existing knowledge to understand new information (Means & Voss, 1985; Scardamalia & Bereiter, 1991). They are able to perceive large, meaningful patterns in their domain; remember things better; try harder to analyze problems; understand problems at a deeper level; and recognize their own conceptual limits (Glaser & Chi, 1988). Experts also are able to predict likely outcomes better than are novices (Chiesi et al., 1979).

Whereas the problems that experts addressed in the research literature were chess games, baseball games, politics, medical diagnoses, and the like, it is intriguing to think that friends might approach personal issues in the same way. It seems plausible that a friend is better able than an acquaintance to connect what he or she is told to what he or she already knew, to see patterns in behavior, to remember more of the story, to try harder to figure out what to do, to understand the problem more deeply, to make good guesses about likely outcomes, and to consider that he or she might be wrong. In short, experts understand their domains more deeply than novices do, and friends, as experts on each other, understand each other better than acquaintances do. This is exactly what we want in friends.

There may be no shortcuts to this process. Unlike computers, which can share huge bodies of information in milliseconds, humans must share talk and/or experiences and this takes time. There is no way around it. Although people may experience "instant intimacy" (as discussed in a later chapter of this series), such intimacy cannot be based on mutual knowledge. It can be based on a strong emotional bond that comes from sharing a powerful experience (such as supporting each other through cancer treatments), but it probably will need to be shored up eventually with more extensive mutual knowledge. People may be brought together by a crisis and yet realize afterward that they feel close but they do not really "know" each other. "Knowing" means developing extensive mutual knowledge and that takes time.

Mutual knowledge, however, need not be complete. One advantage of friendship is that there are domains of knowledge that we do not need because we know our friend has them. Wegner and colleagues (Wegner, 1987; Wegner, Giuliano, & Hertel, 1985; Wegner, Raymond, & Erber, 1991) have investigated the phenomenon of "transactive memory" and have found that intimate pairs specialize in different domains of knowledge and rely on each other's expertise. For instance, one friend might be the movie expert and another might be the music expert and each can get good recommendations from the other's domain without having to become expert him- or herself.

How Mutual Knowledge Continues to Haunt

Many of the advantages that mutual knowledge gives friends become disadvantages when relationships end. Transactive memory, for instance, is wonderful to have and terrible to lose (Wegner et al., 1985). If you lose your friend, you may lose his or her knowledge of film or of how to jump-start your car. You may be able to regain this knowledge by learning about film or by finding someone else who knows how to jump-start your car. What cannot be replaced, however, are your joint connections to the past. He or she was the only one there when you celebrated the birth of your daughter and he or she is the only person who knows how you felt. You cannot reminisce about that event with anyone else, so a part of your past is lost when you lose that friendship.

Investment models of relationships emphasize resources that are sunk into relationships and make people disinclined to give up their investments, hoping instead that they may pay off in the longer run. Surely the time devoted to cultivating mutual knowledge is one of those investments. At the end of a friendship, it is hard to imagine starting over again with a new friend—telling him or her about your childhood, your passion for music, your mother's psychological problems, and your formative years in the Peace Corps. It seems an overwhelming task and, as indicated earlier, there probably are no shortcuts. Regardless of other types of difficulties in friendships, investments in mutual knowledge usually do pay off in efficiency, accuracy, and depth of communication and that is valuable. It must be weighed carefully along with other rewards and costs.

Not only does the loss of mutual knowledge have important cognitive effects, but it has emotional consequences as well. Wood (1986) makes a persuasive argument that the essence of loneliness is "failed intersubjectivity." Loneliness does not come from being alone; it comes from a lack of shared understanding and lack of taken-for-granted meanings. Wood argues that the typical definition of loneliness is a discrepancy between desired and actual quantity or quality of personal relationships, but that definition does not capture situations in which a person is frustrated, angry, or disappointed in a relationship, but not lonely. Only when someone feels a gulf of separateness does he or she feel lonely. This also explains why we may feel especially lonely when we are surrounded by people with whom we share little knowledge and few assumptions about the world. Wood (1986) suggests that it may be difficult for people to describe their feeling of loneliness "precisely because it encompasses the unarticulated, the taken-for-granted" (p. 189).

All this presumes that in failed relationships, mutual knowledge either was lost or was never developed adequately. That may not be true. Partners may have had a great deal of mutual knowledge and mutual understanding but the relationship failed for other reasons. In that case, mutual knowledge may come back to haunt when it is most unwelcome. After all, a former intimate knows many of the same secrets that a current intimate knows, and that can be uncomfortable. Just as mutual knowledge cannot be created immediately, it cannot be destroyed immediately either. It must wither away. In many ways, you can go backward in relationships. You can choose not to be open, not to trust, not to care, but you cannot choose not to know. You can stop developing mutual knowledge, you can let the knowledge become out-of-date, but you cannot make it go away.

Or you can become enemies. One of the best known fictional pair of enemies is Sherlock Holmes and Professor Moriarty. Certainly, they are not close in the everyday sense of liking or loving one another, but they do have a great deal of mutual knowledge about their shared cases, about the events surrounding the cases, and about each other. In some ways, no one knows Holmes as well as Moriarty does and no one knows Moriarty as well as Holmes does. Perhaps some people cling to enemies because there is a worse alternative: loneliness. Perhaps being hated is better than being misunderstood or estranged. One can imagine Holmes and Moriarty after their careers are over, sitting by the fire in an old folks' home, reminiscing about their common adventures.

Friends as Experts on Each Other

Throughout this chapter we have argued that we must look at mutual knowledge in order to understand basic communication processes and, especially, to understand how people in close relationships communicate with one another. Our analysis has dealt primarily with how people develop and use mutual knowledge, rather than with why they do so. We leave the "why" questions to theories of attraction, social exchange, relationship development, or other frameworks that attempt to explain why some people become close friends, others become enemies, others pass pleasant but limited time together, and still others converse and walk away, never to see each other again. Mutual knowledge plays a role in conversations regardless of the level of closeness of the participants, but it plays a very different role for acquaintances than it does for friends, as we have illustrated with examples throughout this chapter.

Thinking of friends as experts on each other captures many of the important differences between how friends use mutual knowledge and how acquaintances do. Friends know a great deal about each other and use their knowledge almost constantly in conversation. They are able to talk more efficiently and to comprehend more deeply than acquaintances and it shows in their talk. By contrast, acquaintances have to either discover or develop mutual knowledge before they can converse efficiently. That is at least one of the reasons that friends are so valuable to us.

Consistent with the themes of this series, we have seen that developing and using mutual knowledge in conversation are both a skill and a process. Exceptionally skilled social actors are able to ask questions or bring up topics to tap into shared knowledge. They are able to remember what knowledge they do or do not share with others and to use it appropriately in conversation. They are able to keep up-to-date with the lives of all the people they know and all the events in the world that might be discussed. They are able to handle gracefully situations in which they share a great deal of mutual knowledge with one person and very little with another. They are able to rely on friends for information just enough to be efficient but not so much as to be debilitated if the friendship ends. They even know enough about their enemies to make the struggle interesting.

No one is as skilled as all that, but fortunately most of us develop adequate skill in the ongoing process of learning about the world and about each other. Simply being together and talking with another person almost necessarily build mutual knowledge, and the process gains momentum as we go along. The more we find that we have in common, the more we have to talk about and experience together, then the more we have in common, and so on throughout the continuing process of building a relationship. The more we know about someone, the easier it is to learn more, which deepens our knowledge further, and so on. This is at least part of the process through which friends help us understand ourselves, keep us informed about the world, and join with us in a bond of shared experience.

2

The Intrapersonal-Interpersonal Dialectical Process of Self-Disclosure

Kathryn Dindia

S idney Jourard (1971), pioneer of theory and research on self-disclosure, proclaimed, "Man has to be willing to show himself" (p. 16). Self-disclosure, defined as "what individuals verbally reveal about themselves to others (including thoughts, feelings, and experiences)" (Derlega, Metts, Petronio, & Margulis, 1993, p. 1), sounds simple, and indeed it would be simple if self-disclosure were an act. But self-disclosure is a process, and processes are always more complicated than acts. In this chapter I review three perspectives on self-disclosure: self-disclosure viewed as an act, self-disclosure viewed as an interpersonal process, and self-disclosure viewed as an intrapersonal process. I argue that because self-disclosure is both an intrapersonal and an interpersonal process, rather than merely an act, it requires considerably more knowledge and skill than is implied by the act perspective on self-disclosure. In addition, I argue that

AUTHOR'S NOTE: I thank Lee West for introducing me to the intrapersonal process perspective on self-disclosure and Jack Johnson and Steve Duck for their helpful editing of earlier drafts of this chapter.

the intrapersonal and interpersonal processes of self-disclosure
interface with one another and are inherently dialectical in nature.
The view that self-disclosure is an intrapersonal-interpersonal
dialectical process is important to the dynamics of relationships,
both in the long term (relational development and maintenance)
and in the short term (interaction dynamics of self-disclosure).

Self-Disclosure as an Act

Jourard was among the first to conceptualize self-disclosure as
an act. "Self-disclosure is the *act* of making yourself manifest,
showing yourself so others can perceive you" (Jourard, 1971,
p. 19, italics added). Research that examines self-disclosure from
an act perspective focuses on an individual's messages or acts (of
self-disclosure) and attempts to identify the causes and effects
of the act of self-disclosure. The unit of analysis is the act (Cline,
1983), and typical research variables include intimacy, amount,
valence, accuracy, clarity, and flexibility of self-disclosure (Cline,
1982).

According to this perspective, the causes of the act of self-disclosure rest in the individual. This approach led to the study of
self-disclosure as a personality trait or construct. As a personality trait, self-disclosure is viewed as an enduring characteristic
or attribute of an individual. An individual's "ability" and "willingness" to self-disclose have been studied. Studies cast within
this perspective attempt to identify high and low disclosers (by
designing measures of self-disclosure as a personality trait) and
to correlate individual differences in self-disclosure with demo-
graphic and biological characteristics (sex, age, race, religion,
birth order), sociocultural differences, and other personality
traits (Archer, 1979).

Sex is the individual difference variable that has been studied
most. More than 200 studies involving more than 27,000 subjects
have been conducted on gender differences in self-disclosure.
Although most people believe there are large gender differences
in self-disclosure, a recent meta-analysis of this research (Dindia

& Allen, 1992) found that gender differences in self-disclosure are small (approximately $d = .20$, $r = .10$). By small I mean that one needs a statistical analysis to detect gender differences in self-disclosure; you cannot see the difference with your eyes. In this respect, gender differences in self-disclosure are similar to the difference in height between 15- and 16-year-old girls. If the effect size for gender differences in self-disclosure represented the probability that females versus males would disclose a particular item of information, such as their most embarrassing moment, then 56% of females would disclose this information, whereas only 44% of men would disclose it.

Although gender differences are small, Dindia and Allen concluded that gender differences are generalizable to both self-disclosure to strangers and self-disclosure to partners with whom one has a personal relationship (i.e., friend, spouse, parent). It also was found that females disclose most to other females. Thus it appears that females self-disclose more and elicit more self-disclosure. Again, however, these differences are small. The only medium effect size was for other-report of self-disclosure ($d = .44$). Individuals report that females disclose more to them than males do. Why is there a medium effect size for other-report of self-disclosure (and only a small effect for self-report and observational studies of gender differences in self-disclosure)? Dindia and Allen (1992) hypothesized that this is the result of a stereotype: We tend to believe that females disclose more than males do, so when asked, we report that females disclose more to us than males do.

Like the results for gender differences in self-disclosure, the results of studies viewing self-disclosure as an individual difference variable have been inconsistent, and the magnitude of personality differences in self-disclosure generally small. In reviewing the research on individual differences in self-disclosure, Archer (1979) states that "no categorical picture of the high discloser emerges from the personality research" and that a "hazy, confused portrait is all that can be distilled from some twenty years of research" (pp. 37-38). The same is true today.

From this "act" perspective the consequences of self-disclosure are viewed as uniformly positive. Self-disclosure is viewed as a necessary and good behavior (Cline, 1983). According to Jourard (1971), mental and physical health as well as personal development can be attained only through the act of self-disclosure: "No man can come to know himself except as an outcome of disclosing himself to another person" (p. 9), and "Self-disclosure is a symptom of personality health *and* a means of ultimately achieving healthy personality" (p. 32, italics in original). Jourard (1971) claimed that self-disclosure was essential for effective counseling or psychotherapy: "People come to need help because they have not disclosed themselves in some optimum degree to the people in their lives" (p. 29).

The emphasis, from this perspective, has been on facilitating the act of self-disclosure (Bochner, 1982; Cozby, 1973; Parks, 1982). Many interpersonal textbooks and instructors' manuals include exercises for facilitating individuals' willingness to self-disclose and skills in the act of self-disclosure. The resulting pedagogy and research stressed increasing self-disclosure (Cline, 1982, p. 6). "Teachers encouraged openness, honesty, and disclosure. Research emphasized modeling and while many published articles were built on the unstated premise of disclosure holding inherent value, no single study began from the premise that self-disclosure needed to be reduced, alleviated, or eliminated" (Cline, 1983, p. 6). This "ideology of intimacy" prevailed for many years in both teaching and research but recently has been challenged (Bochner, 1982; Cline, 1983; Parks, 1982).

Self-Disclosure as an Interpersonal Process

Self-disclosure is viewed alternatively as an interpersonal process in the personal relationships literature. This perspective assumes that it is the process that occurs when individuals interact with each other, rather than the characteristics of either or both participants, that affects self-disclosure (Pearce & Sharp,

1973). Thus "disclosure should not be categorized into camps of 'those who do' and 'those who don't'" (Gilbert & Horenstein, 1975, p. 319). This perspective emphasizes reciprocity of self-disclosure; the correlation of self-disclosure and liking; and the role of self-disclosure in the development, maintenance, and dissolution of relationships (Berg & Derlega, 1987). From this perspective of self-disclosure, the relationship, rather than the individual, and the interact(ion), rather than the act, are the focus of study.

Reciprocity of Self-Disclosure

Jourard (1971) originated the idea that self-disclosure is reciprocal: "In ordinary social relationships, disclosure is a reciprocal phenomenon. Participants in dialogue disclose their thoughts, feelings, actions, etc., to the other and are disclosed to in return. I called this reciprocity the 'dyadic effect': disclosure begets disclosure" (p. 66). Several theories have been used to predict and explain reciprocity of self-disclosure (see Chelune, 1979, for a review and discussion of these theories), including liking and attraction, trust, social exchange, and primarily the norm of reciprocity (Gouldner, 1960).

Reciprocity of self-disclosure has been tested a number of ways, the most common being the correlation between two persons' self-disclosure (Hill & Stull, 1982). A review of the literature (Dindia, 1982) found that, in general, partners' reports of self-disclosure are positively related. This is true for both intrasubjective and intersubjective perceptions of self-disclosure. Intrasubjective perceptions refer to the perceptions of one person. Specifically, they refer to the correlation between a subject's perception of his or her self-disclosure to a partner and the subject's perception of the partner's self-disclosure to the subject (disclosure received). Intersubjective perceptions are perceptions between persons. They refer to the correlation between a subject's perception of his or her self-disclosure to a partner and the partner's perception of his or her self-disclosure to the subject. The review of literature (Dindia, 1982) also indicates that there is a positive relationship between dyad partners' and small group members' observed self-disclosure.

A criticism leveled against this test of reciprocity is that it confuses base rates of self-disclosure with reciprocity of self-disclosure. For example, two persons' levels of self-disclosure may be related due to similar personality traits (e.g., Kate and John are both high or low disclosers) rather than being due to Kate's self-disclosure eliciting John's self-disclosure and vice versa. Correlation confounds individual differences in self-disclosure with reciprocity of self-disclosure.

A second test of reciprocity of self-disclosure is whether an experimenter's or confederate's self-disclosure has a positive effect on a subject's self-disclosure. A review of the literature (Dindia, 1982) found that, in general, a confederate's or experimenter's self-disclosure has a positive effect on a subject's reported intention to disclose and actual self-disclosure. However, the generalizability of these results has been seriously questioned. An experimenter's or confederate's self-disclosure may have a positive effect on a subject's self-disclosure, but these results may not be externally valid. "Investigators have used superficial, perfunctory remarks in the low disclosure condition and explicit, personal comments on highly private topics . . . for the high disclosure conditions" (Chelune, 1979, p. 14).

Sequential analysis also has been used to test reciprocity of self-disclosure. Whether Kate's self-disclosure elicits John's self-disclosure in the subsequent turn (or near subsequent turn), and vice versa, is tested. Dindia (1982, 1988) and Spencer (1993c) found that such a pattern of reciprocity of self-disclosure is not exhibited in conversations. However, there is a problem using sequential analysis to test reciprocity of self-disclosure. An individual may reciprocate self-disclosure at a later point in the conversation, or even in a later conversation.

The dyadic effect is assumed to be a time-bound process in which people mutually regulate their disclosure to one another, at some agreed-on pace. But little more is said about temporal aspects of reciprocity. The rate at which it occurs, how it ebbs and flows, and factors that accelerate or retard reciprocity of exchange are not discussed in detail (Altman, 1973, p. 250).

Thus reciprocity of self-disclosure may occur in a manner other than one person's self-disclosure increasing the probability of the partner's self-disclosure in the subsequent turn (or near subsequent turn). Reciprocity of self-disclosure may not occur on a tit-for-tat basis ("My most embarrassing moment was . . ." "My most embarrassing moment was . . ."). It may be that an individual's self-disclosure has a positive effect on his or her partner's self-disclosure, and vice versa, in some general sense that is not manifested on a turn-by-turn basis.

Miller and Kenny (1986) provide a solution to the problem of testing reciprocity of self-disclosure. Miller and Kenny differentiated two types of reciprocity of self-disclosure: individual reciprocity and dyadic reciprocity. Individual reciprocity refers to the extent to which individuals who generally disclose are generally disclosed to. Thus individual reciprocity refers to individual differences in self-disclosure. Dyadic reciprocity refers to self-disclosure that is unique to the particular relationship, controlling for individual differences in self-disclosure. Dyadic reciprocity refers to the extent to which people adjust their unique disclosure to their partner (how much they disclose to their partner above or below how much they disclose in general). Of all the tests of reciprocity of self-disclosure, Miller and Kenny's dyadic reciprocity most closely matches Jourard's conceptual definition of reciprocity of self-disclosure.

Miller and Kenny (1986) studied individual and dyadic reciprocity using social relations analysis. They asked sorority women to indicate how much they disclosed to and received disclosure from all other sorority sisters. The results indicated that reciprocity of self-disclosure, for both intrasubjective and intersubjective perceptions of self-disclosure, existed only at the dyadic level. There was no individual reciprocity; that is, people who generally disclosed were not generally disclosed to. In another study using social relations analysis, dyadic reciprocity of self-reported self-disclosure was nonsignificant (Wright &

Ingraham, 1986), but dyadic reciprocity of actual self-disclosure within conversations was significant (Wright & Ingraham, 1985).

A third study using social relations analysis (Dindia, Fitzpatrick, & Kenny, 1989) examined dyadic reciprocity in conversations between same- and opposite-sex strangers. In general, strangers reciprocated high-intimacy self-disclosure within conversations. Same-sex strangers reciprocated low-intimacy evaluative self-disclosure (feelings, opinions, and judgments); however, opposite-sex strangers did not reciprocate low-intimacy evaluative self-disclosure. Neither same- nor opposite-sex strangers reciprocated low-intimacy descriptive self-disclosure (information and facts about self). On the one hand, this seems paradoxical because typically it is hypothesized that reciprocity of low-intimacy descriptive (e.g., "My name is . . . ," "My name is . . . ," "My major is . . . ," "My major is . . . ") information drives initial interactions between strangers. On the other hand, if both people are following the same script for initial interaction between strangers, which prescribes that they provide low-intimacy descriptive information about themselves, it makes sense that descriptive self-disclosure is not reciprocal. Partners in initial interaction may not be reciprocating descriptive self-disclosure; they may be disclosing information and facts about themselves independently of one another.

Altman (1973) hypothesized that reciprocity of self-disclosure decreases as a relationship develops. Hill and Stull (1982) argued that reciprocity does not decrease as a relationship develops but that the time frame over which reciprocity may occur increases. Regardless, strangers should reciprocate self-disclosure within conversations more than spouses.

Morton (1978) studied the effect of level of relationship on reciprocity of self-disclosure and did not find a significant main effect of level of relationship (spouse vs. stranger) on reciprocity of self-disclosure. However, Morton found a significant interaction effect of level of relationship and time interval (conversations were divided into three equal time intervals). Strangers demonstrated a stable level of reciprocity across the conversation, whereas married couples demonstrated an initially equivalent degree of reciprocity and then gradually decreased their reciprocity over the course of the conversation. Morton speculated that initial exposure to the novel experimental situation may have prompted spouses to return temporarily to a norm of reciprocity, but then to gradually abandon this as familiar dyad-specific interaction patterns reemerged.

Dindia et al. (1989) also studied reciprocity of self-disclosure between spouses. Spouses engaged in three dyadic conversations, at 1-week intervals. Dindia et al. found that spouses reciprocated high-intimacy self-disclosure but not low-intimacy self-disclosure within conversations. The authors speculated that spouses may not reciprocate low-intimacy self-disclosure because low-intimacy self-disclosure may not count as self-disclosure in more developed relationships and, thus, may not be governed by norms of reciprocity. More important, Dindia et al. (1989) found that reciprocity in spouse conversations was not significantly less than reciprocity in stranger conversations. This is in contrast to the general hypothesis that strangers should reciprocate self-disclosure more than spouses. Dindia et al. (1989) also examined whether reciprocity of self-disclosure for spouses decreased from the first to the third session. There was no consistent trend of decreasing reciprocity across occasions. Unlike the spouses in Morton's sample, spouses did not decrease the level of within-conversation reciprocity as they became more familiar with the experimental setting.

The results of research on reciprocity of self-disclosure tend to be overwhelming and at times confusing. However, reviewing these results is important for understanding the skills of reciprocity of self-disclosure. First, "reciprocity is 'normative,' meaning it is a common and expected occurrence but is not invariant or automatic" (Derlega et al., 1993). More specifically, the various statistical tests tell us that self-disclosure is generally reciprocal, that it is generally perceived as being reciprocal, and that reciprocity generally occurs within conversations, perhaps even in developed relationships.

But reciprocity of self-disclosure does not occur on a tit-for-tat basis. Strangers, "for whom judgments of competence rest on displays of normative behavior and for whom small tests of trustworthiness need to be assessed quickly" (Derlega et al., 1993, p. 35), should be most likely to reciprocate self-disclosure on a tit-for-tat basis. However, research indicates that strangers do not reciprocate self-disclosure on a tit-for-tat basis. Friends, and partners in other developed relationships, should be less likely to reciprocate disclosure on a tit-for-tat basis because "there is less need to reciprocate intimate self-disclosure immediately and during the same interaction" (Derlega et al., 1993, p. 35). In support of this, Derlega, Wilson, and Chaikin (1976) found that subjects reciprocated self-disclosure to a note they thought was from a stranger but they did not reciprocate self-disclosure when they thought the note was from a friend (in both cases the note was actually from an experimental confederate). However, these results contrast with the results of Dindia et al. (1989), who found that spouses, as well as strangers, reciprocate high-intimacy self-disclosure within conversations.

In sum, the interpersonally competent response to self-disclosure may not be to immediately reciprocate self-disclosure. As Berg and Archer (1980) note, "Informal observations suggest that self-disclosures are met with a variety of responses. Indeed, a common reaction to hearing about an intimate problem in another's life is to express concern or empathy" (pp. 246-247). Berg and Archer (1980) argued that a more flexible view of the reciprocity norm might allow the recipient of self-disclosure to acknowledge the self-disclosure and express interest or concern with its content in lieu of responding with self-disclosure. Thus intimacy, rather than self-disclosure, is reciprocated. Berg and Archer conducted an experiment in which they examined subjects' perceptions of an individual based on the individual's response to a self-disclosure. Berg and Archer (1980) found that the most favorable impressions of the respondent were formed when the respondent expressed concern for a discloser rather than when the respondent returned any level of self-disclosure.

Alternatively, Dindia (1984) found that self-disclosure, rather than being reciprocal, was followed sequentially by acknowledgments (such as "mm-hmm," "oh," and "yeah"). Perhaps, rather than reciprocating self-disclosure, at least immediately, the most desirable response is to acknowledge self-disclosure; that is, to respond in a way that shows you are listening and that it is okay to continue self-disclosing.

Thus it may be more important to respond to self-disclosure with interest and/or concern, rather than immediately to reciprocate self-disclosure, and to reciprocate self-disclosure later, when it is more appropriate. How soon you reciprocate self-disclosure may depend on the level of the relationship. Strangers and acquaintances, for whom there is no guarantee of a future conversation, may need to reciprocate self-disclosure within conversations in order to develop trust and to ensure that they have a subsequent conversation. Friends and spouses may not need to reciprocate self-disclosure within conversations (although there is some evidence that they still may do so) because trust already is established and because they know there will be future opportunities to reciprocate self-disclosure.

Self-Disclosure and Liking

Self-disclosure and liking are thought to be related in at least three ways: self-disclosure leads to liking, liking leads to disclosure, and we like another as a result of having disclosed to him or her. The effect of a person's self-disclosure on a partner's liking for the person who discloses has been of greatest theoretical interest, and studies examining this effect make up the bulk of the studies on self-disclosure and liking (Collins & Miller, 1993). This effect typically is referred to as the "disclosure-liking hypothesis." A recent meta-analysis of the disclosure/liking relationship (Collins & Miller, 1993) confirms that we like people who self-disclose to us, we disclose more to people we like, and we like others as a result of having disclosed to them. However, there are several qualifications to the disclosure/liking relationship.

First, the degree of correlation between self-disclosure and liking may be overestimated. Bochner (1982) noted that people tend to believe it is appropriate to engage in high amounts of self-disclosure with others they like, so when asked, they report that they engage in higher disclosure to persons they like. This does not mean that people actually self-disclose more to others they like. Similarly, Bochner (1982) pointed out that people over-estimate the extent to which they self-disclose to others they like and that this, too, would artificially increase the correlation between self-disclosure and liking. Support for this was found in the meta-analysis of self-disclosure and liking. Collins and Miller (1993) found that the mean effect for the relationship between self-disclosure and liking was significantly greater for correlational studies (which are self-report studies) than the mean effect for experimental studies (which are observational studies). A large effect was found for correlational (self-report) studies, whereas small effects were found for experimental (observational) studies.

Second, disclosure that violates normative expectations will not lead to liking. Specifically, self-disclosure that is too intimate or too negative will not lead to liking (Bochner, 1982; Derlega et al., 1993; Parks, 1982). In initial interaction it is normative to engage in low-intimacy descriptive self-disclosure that reflects positively on oneself. Any self-disclosure that deviates from this norm may produce negative attributions (Bochner, 1982). However, Collins and Miller (1993) did not find evidence that high disclosure leads to less liking relative to low disclosure in their meta-analysis of self-disclosure and liking, although they indicate that their finding is limited given the small number of studies on which the finding was based ($N = 7$) and the difficulty in comparing disclosure levels from one study to the next.

It is generally expected that self-disclosure should mutually and gradually become more intimate as a relationship develops. However, even in intimate relationships, people should be wary of disclosing negative information about self, partner (giving negative feedback), or the relationship. There are norms about what is appropriate for discussion even in developed relationships. Taboo topics are topics that are "off limits" to relationship partners (Baxter & Wilmot, 1985). Results of a study of opposite-sex friendships, romantic relationships, and relationships that had the potential to become romantic indicated six primary types of taboo topics: the state of the relationship, extra-relationship activity, relationship norms, prior relationships with opposite-sex partners, conflict-inducing topics, and negatively valanced self-disclosures (Baxter & Wilmot, 1985). Although no research has specifically tested whether the disclosure of taboo topics negatively affects attraction, there is research indicating that the disclosure of negatively valanced information does (Gilbert & Horenstein, 1975). As Bochner (1982) states, "The research we have reviewed indicates that discriminating disclosers are more satisfied and more likely to remain attractive to their partners than are indiscriminating disclosers" (p. 120).

The third qualification to the disclosure/liking relationship is that high disclosers are not liked more than low disclosers. In a study on the relationship between self-disclosure and liking, L. C. Miller (1990) asked sorority women to indicate how much they disclosed to, received disclosure from, and liked each other. Individuals who generally disclosed more to others were not liked more by others. However, individuals who disclosed more to a particular partner than they generally disclosed to others were liked more by that partner. This was true for both intrasubjective and intersubjective perceptions. Thus there was a positive relationship between a subject's reported liking of a partner and the subject's perceptions of the partner's unique self-disclosure to the subject. Similarly, there was a positive relationship between a subject's report of his or her unique self-disclosure to a partner and the partner's reported liking of the subject.

Berg and Derlega (1987) noted that people make attributions regarding another person's disclosure and that "the attributions we use to explain why someone is telling us something intimate or revealing are an important part of what the self-disclosure will mean to the relationship" (Derlega et al., 1993, p. 27). People can attribute another person's self-disclosure to the person's disposition or personality (he or she disclosed to me because he or she is generally an open person) or to their relationship (he or she disclosed to me because we have a special relationship). When we perceive another person's self-disclosure as personalistic (revealed only to the target) rather than nonpersonalistic (revealed to many people), research indicates that it leads to increased liking (Berg & Derlega, 1987). In support of this, the Collins and Miller (1993) meta-analysis of the disclosure/liking relationship found that the mean effect size for self-disclosure where a personalistic attribution was made was $d = .453$ ($r = .221$), and the mean effect size for nonpersonalistic attributions was $d = .228$ ($r = .113$). Although the difference was not statistically significant, it was in the predicted direction. Collins and Miller (1993) concluded that "these studies provide some evidence that the relation between disclosure and liking may be stronger if the recipient believes that the disclosure was given because of something unique or special about him- or herself" (p. 20).

The results of research on the disclosure/liking relationship have important theoretical implications for self-disclosure viewed as a personality trait (the "act" perspective) versus self-disclosure viewed as an interpersonal process. Specifically, this research lends support to the importance of viewing self-disclosure as an interpersonal process, rather than merely as an act. Similarly, these results have important practical applications for the skills of self-disclosure. They indicate that we should not encourage people to self-disclose more in general. High disclosers are not liked more by others than are low disclosers. Certainly we need to be able to engage in intimate self-disclosure with someone we like or someone whom we want to like us, but it is important that self-disclosure be appropriate to the situation and the relationship, be particular to the partner, and be perceived as being particular to the partner.

Thus research on self-disclosure and liking indicates that disclosure leads to liking as long as the disclosure is appropriate and, in particular, as long as self-disclosure is not too intimate or too negative. Similarly, this research indicates that we should not disclose more in general to be liked more by others. It is only when we disclose information to a particular partner that liking increases.

Self-Disclosure and Relationship Development

According to early theory on relationship development, in particular, social penetration theory (Altman & Taylor, 1973), self-disclosure was synonymous with relationship development. Self-disclosure was viewed as the cause and effect of relationship development (and consequently was used as a measure of relationship development). More recently self-disclosure has been viewed as one component in the development of a relationship. "Although self-disclosure is not equivalent to and does not define the level of intimacy of a relationship, it is one major factor in the development, maintenance, and deterioration of a relationship" (Derlega et al., 1993, p. ix).

Self-disclosure is an important component in the initiation of a relationship:

> Imagine that you have just been introduced to someone at a party. What do you say to one another? You may talk about the music or the people at the party. You are not yet willing to self-disclose. But if you discover that this person has observations or opinions that are similar to your own or if you are attracted for other reasons, you may begin to tell this person things about yourself (what you are taking at school or where you come from) and to ask him or her questions. Soon you know something about your new acquaintance and he or she knows something about you. You have begun to self-disclose to one another. It is hard to imagine how a relationship might get started without such self-disclosure. (Derlega et al., 1993, pp. 1-2)

Self-disclosure is important for people to get to know each other. According to uncertainty-reduction theory (Berger & Calabrese, 1975), as we reduce our uncertainty about another we obtain predictive and explanatory knowledge about another. This acquisition of knowledge (or reduction in uncertainty) causes an increase in liking, intimacy of information, nonverbal affiliative expressiveness, and amount of verbal communication. All of these factors contribute to the escalation of a relationship.

Through self-disclosure we also acquire mutual knowledge or knowledge that two people share, know they share, and use in interacting with one another (see Planalp & Garvin-Doxas, Chapter 1 in this volume). Although Planalp and Garvin-Doxas argue that acquaintance talk is founded on mutual knowledge, not on self-disclosure, self-disclosure is important for establishing mutual knowledge and vice versa.

Self-disclosure is also an important component in the development of a relationship. According to Derlega et al. (1993):

> If you like this person, you will want to know more about him or her, and you will, in turn, be willing to share more information about yourself. You will begin to talk about attitudes, feelings, and personal experiences; in brief, you will begin to disclose more personal information. If your new friend likes you, he or she also will disclose personal information. (p. 2)

Social-penetration theory argues that social depenetration is the reverse of social penetration (Altman & Taylor, 1973). According to this theory, breadth and depth of self-disclosure gradually and incrementally decrease as a relationship declines and terminates. Except for one study, research supports the proposition that depth of disclosure reverses as a relationship declines (see Baxter, 1987). However, studies on the reversal of breadth of disclosure are few and the results are inconsistent (Baxter, 1987).

Relational Dialectics

In early scholarly and nonscholarly literature regarding self-disclosure, openness was advocated; in later literature, closedness was valued (Kidd, 1975). The most recent scholarly and nonscholarly literature takes a dialectic approach to the issue of self-disclosure and privacy regulation (Prusank, Duran, & DeLillo, 1993). Similarly, I argue that the interpersonal process of self-disclosure is dialectical in nature and that it is this dialectical nature of self-disclosure that is important to the dynamics of self-disclosure and relationships.

According to relational dialectics, relationships are viewed as involving contradictory and opposing tensions. A dialectical perspective views contradictions not only as persistent in interpersonal relationships, but also as essential to the development of close interpersonal bonds (Baxter, 1988; Rawlins, 1983). There are four essential tenets of the dialectical perspective (Montgomery, 1993):

1. Oppositional forces form the basis of all social phenomena including social relationships.
2. Change is constant in such phenomena.
3. Social relationships are defined by relations among their characteristics.
4. Dialectical tensions are never eliminated, but they may be transformed, adapted to, and managed.

Several dialectical theorists/researchers have posited openness-closedness or expressiveness-protectiveness as a dialectical tension in relationships (Altman, Vinsel, & Brown, 1981; Baxter, 1988; Rawlins, 1983). According to this perspective, relationships need both information openness and information closedness, requiring decisions to reveal and conceal personal information (Rawlins, 1983). Rawlins states that individuals must continually face the contradictory impulses to be open and expressive and to be protective of self and/or of other. Mutual expressiveness is necessary to achieve intimacy but self-disclosure opens areas of vulnerability, and to avoid hurting each other people must undertake protective measures (Rawlins, 1983). Thus "protectiveness is the dialectical necessity of expressiveness. . . . An individual must continually confront the contradictory inclinations to be open and expressive *and* to be protective of self and other" (Rawlins, 1983, p. 5, italics in original).

Individuals can respond to the dialectical tension of openness-closedness with a number of strategic responses (Baxter, 1990). Baxter (1990), in a study of the existence of and responses to dialectical tensions in relationships, found that the most dominant strategy reported for the openness-closedness contradiction was segmentation, followed by moderation and selection. Segmentation involved a differentiation of the topic domains into those for which self-disclosure was appropriate and those regarded as taboo topics. Moderation typically manifested itself in the proverbial small-talk ritual, in which respondents engaged in superficial to modest self-disclosure yet maintained moderate discretion. Selection could take the form of total openness (more common) or total withholding of information from the other (less common). Satisfaction did not correlate significantly with the perceived existence of the openness-closedness tension in the relationship. Instead, relational satisfaction was negatively related with the use of disqualification (indirect strategies to reveal self and acquire information about the other person) for the openness-closedness contradiction.

Rawlins's (1983) research on the dialectics of expressiveness and protectiveness illustrates the complicated interpersonal process of self-disclosure from a dialectical perspective. Rawlins defined expressiveness as including revealing personal aspects of oneself to another as well as commenting about another's individual qualities. Rawlins found two conversational dilemmas resulting from the contradictory impulses to be open and expressive and to be protective of self and/or of other. Specifically, the dialectical coexistence of expressiveness and protectiveness engender dilemmas of diagnosis and strategy in the decision of whether to self-disclose (Rawlins, 1983). An individual confronts the contradictory dilemma of protecting self by restricting personal disclosure and of striving to be open by confiding in other. Disclosing personal information to another makes one susceptible to hurt by the other. The decision to self-disclose will be a function of at least two things: an individual's perceived need to be open about a given issue and the individual's trust of the partner's discretion (his or her abilities to keep a secret and exercise restraint regarding self's sensitivities). The decision to reveal or conceal involves assessing what will be gained or lost by either choice (Rawlins, 1983).

Dilemmas of diagnosis and strategy also confront an individual deciding whether to disclose statements regarding other. The decision to disclose will be a function of the self's perceived need to be honest about a given issue and the amount of restraint appropriate to the topic. An individual develops an awareness of topics that make the other vulnerable to hurt or anger. In particular *"self must determine whether telling the truth is worth causing the other pain and breaching the other's trust in self's protective inclinations"* (Rawlins, 1983, p. 10, italics in original).

The dialectical perspective paints a more complicated picture of the skills involved in competent self-disclosure. From the dialectical perspective, competent self-disclosure is that which is responsive to partners' needs for intimacy and privacy. Rawlins's (1983) analysis suggests that "it may be equally important for an individual to develop skill at restrained remarks and selective disclosure of private information" (p. 13). "An apt handling of the dialectic [of expressiveness and protectiveness] means that self limits self's own vulnerability and strives to protect other while still expressing thoughts and feelings" (Rawlins, 1983, p. 5). Rawlins's (1983) analysis also suggests that competent communication is more than skillful behavior; one must possess skills of diagnosis (know when to use expressiveness vs. protectiveness) and skills of strategy (the ability to be open or expressive and closed or protective). From a dialectical perspective (Rawlins, 1983), "we cannot mandate a specific style for relational interaction and scholars should be cautious in stressing open communication as the hallmark of intimacy" (p. 13). Instead:

> This perspective urges teaching students to behave strategically with regard to desired relational goals, rather than simply with regard to personal goals. When students learn about self-disclosure from this view, they think about the impact of their disclosures on the definition of their relationship. Hence, the value of disclosure can be assessed not only in terms of personal risks, but also in terms of relational risks. (Cline, 1983, p. 4)

Theory and research on self-disclosure from the interpersonal-process perspective indicate that, in general, self-disclosure is reciprocal, it causes liking, and it plays a role in relationship development. However, there are important qualifications to all of the above conclusions, qualifications that often go overlooked and that have important ramifications for the skills of self-disclosure. Specifically, the interpersonal perspective on self-disclosure acknowledges, and emphasizes in dialectical approaches, that self-disclosure can have negative, as well as positive, effects on a relationship. Thus competent communication is more than an ability to self-disclose; one must know when to self-disclose and when not to self-disclose and must be able to self-disclose and not self-disclose.

Self-Disclosure
as an Intrapersonal Process

This perspective is among the most recent and innovative perspectives on self-disclosure. It originates not in communication or psychology but in the fields of medicine, nursing, and social work. It is based on applied, rather than theoretical, research. This perspective views self-disclosure as an intrapersonal process with definable phases and characteristics, rather than as a single act (Sorenson & Snow, 1991). According to this perspective, self-disclosure is a complex process of moving from nondisclosure to disclosure. Instead of disclosure being viewed as an act, disclosure is more accurately understood as the gradual and incremental process that one goes through from the starting point of negation to full disclosure.

Research on the disclosure of stigmatizing conditions, such as homosexuality, family violence, AIDS and HIV infection, and herpes, has posited a "stigmatization-disclosure process" (Limandri, 1989). In a qualitative analysis of 29 interviews of disclosure of women's abuse, AIDS or HIV antibodies, and herpes, Limandri (1989) found that disclosure of stigmatizing conditions was a process not an act:

> On the surface, disclosure seemed to be a dichotomous variable composed of disclosure or concealment. However, with further examination of the interviews, there appeared to be smaller categories of disclosure. Furthermore, there was a timing aspect of the disclosure in that some would conceal for a while, disclose, then retract back into concealment. . . . [T]here seemed to be an unlayering process to disclosure. (p. 73)

Similarly, Marks et al. (1992) state that learning that one is infected with HIV is a profound emotional experience accompanied with psychological reactions including fear of death and dying, uncertainty about the illness and its treatment, fear of social rejection and isolation, and loss of self-esteem. "These psychological states are not likely to promote disclosure. Rather, disclosure is more likely to occur with greater adjustment to one's disease, and the sheer passage of time may contribute to that adjustment" (Marks et al., 1992, p. 301). Similarly, Gard (1990) suggests that "delaying disclosure reflects a psychological adaptive process" (p. 253).

Although the term *dialectics* is never used, these researchers are, in effect, positing a dialectical model of the intrapersonal process of disclosure of stigmatizing conditions. The dialectical process is due to the fact that stigmatizing conditions contribute to feelings of shame and the wish to conceal or hide; however, those who experience such conditions often need to confide in others and to seek help from professionals (Limandri, 1989). Limandri (1989) describes the dialectical nature of disclosure of stigmatizing conditions:

> To perceive her/his condition as stigmatizing, an individual experiences an underlying feeling of shame. The notion of hiding or concealment is intrinsic to and inseparable from the concept of shame. To avoid shame, the individual must avoid disclosure of the condition. . . . This, however, cannot always be avoided. In fact, the individual may need to disclose her/his stigmatizing condition in order to receive necessary health care. (p. 69)

Similarly, Gershman (1983) described the catch-22 of disclosure of homosexuality, stating that people experience anxiety in disclosing their true feelings yet failure to do so engenders the anxiety of not being oneself. Gard (1990) argued that disclosure of HIV infection to parents may involve a similar catch-22.

According to this perspective the process of disclosure of stigmatizing conditions is cyclical rather than linear. Individuals are confronted with the need to tell or to conceal. "This is not a simple decision or a decision that is made only once, but rather the process simulated a swinging gate or valve that could be completely open, completely closed, or partially open" (Limandri, 1989, p. 76). Although movement is generally from concealment to disclosure, it is not a straightforward process. "Disclosure occurs many more times than once, that people can retract their disclosure at times, and that the process can expand and contract over time" (Limandri, 1989, p. 76).

Marks et al. (1992) argued that the stigma, discrimination, and bias associated with HIV/AIDS influences self-disclosure of HIV infection. Disclosure of HIV infection is a reasoned action that follows from the perceived social, psychological, and material consequences of informing others. People with HIV infection evaluate the consequences of informing a particular target person before a disclosure is made. Further, the factors considered in deciding whether to disclose to a particular target (e.g., a parent) differ from the factors considered in deciding whether to disclose to another target (e.g., a sexual partner). For any potential target the decision process may trigger psychological conflict:

> One may feel the need to inform a significant other for purposes of support but may fear rejection from that person. Similarly, one may feel an ethical obligation to inform medical providers (e.g., dentists) but may simultaneously fear that disclosure will result in refusal of services. (Marks et al., 1992, p. 300).

Limandri (1989) states:

> The circumstances for voluntary disclosure must yield sufficient anticipated reward to counterbalance the disesteem and rejection that may result. The stigmatized person struggles with the conflict of the need to reveal due to a concomitant stressor versus the need to conceal due to further stigmatization. (p. 70)

These arguments are reminiscent of Rawlins's research on the dialectics of disclosure in relationships. The difference is that Rawlins's research is cast at the "relationship level"; that is, Rawlins is concerned with the contradictions that are inevitable features of relationships. However, the present perspective is cast at the "individual level" and is concerned with the contradictions that are inevitable features of individuals cognitively dealing with internal conflict. Altman (1993) has argued that dialectical processes apply to different social units engaged in personal relationships including individual participants, interpersonal processes among dyad members, and couple linkages with other social units such as families, friends, and coworkers. Individual dialectics, which Altman labels *intra-individual dialectical processes,* are played out within an individual. "Indeed, one can conceive of dialectical processes of openness/closedness . . . functioning in the minds of individuals in a relationship" (Altman, 1993, p. 28). Similarly, Berger (1993) argued in the first volume of this series that dialectical phenomena in relationships do not necessarily occur at the relational, as opposed to the individual, level of analysis:

> Clearly individuals can and do wrestle with issues concerned with such dialectical poles as interdependence and autonomy in the absence of any interaction with relationship partners or confidants with whom such issues might be discussed. In fact, recent presentations explicating important dialectical poles in relationships in some ways resemble classical discussions of individual experienced conflict, especially conflicts of the approach-avoidance variety. . . . In many instances such conflicts are dealt with within the heads of the individual social actors and not necessarily at the relational level. Individual cognitions about the conflict may be "social" in that they explicitly involve other persons, specifically relationship partners; but these social cognitions and the decisions they affect . . . are clearly individual-level phenomena. (p. 57)

In an independent, yet coincidentally similar, line of research an intrapersonal process model of children's disclosure of sexual abuse has been proposed. The process of children's disclosure of sexual abuse has been described as the "no-maybe-sometimes-yes" syndrome (MacFarlane & Krebs, 1986). Sorenson and Snow (1991) identified the process of children's disclosure of sexual abuse as containing four progressive phases: denial, disclosure (which contains two subphases, tentative and active disclosure), recant, and reaffirm. Denial is defined as the child's initial statement to any individual that he or she had not been sexually abused. Tentative disclosure refers to the child's partial, vague, or vacillating acknowledgment of sexual abuse; active disclosure indicates a personal admission by the child of having been sexually abused. Recant refers to the child's retraction of a previous allegation of abuse. Reaffirm is defined as the child's reassertion of the validity of a previous assertion of sexual abuse that had been recanted. According to this model, children typically begin by denying that they have been sexually abused, which is followed by tentative and then active disclosure. Some children recant and later reaffirm sexual abuse.

Therapists and social workers involved with sexually abused children claim that denial and ambiguity (i.e., tentative disclosure) are inherent to the process of children's disclosure of sexual abuse. Specifically, sexual abuse creates feelings of fear, helplessness, hopelessness, shame, confusion, isolation, and self-blame in children (Summit, 1983). Children's denial of sexual abuse and recanting of abuse are attempts to shield themselves and their families from negative evaluation and consequences (MacFarlane & Krebs, 1986; Summit, 1983).

Sorensen and Snow (1991) tested their model of the disclosure process in a qualitative analysis of 116 case studies involving sexually abused children from 3 to 17 years of age who eventually were confirmed as credible victims. The results were that 72% of the children initially denied having been sexually abused. Denial was most common when (a) children were initially questioned by a concerned parent or adult authority figure and (b) children were identified as potential victims and initially questioned in a formal investigative interview. Tentative disclosure was the common middle stage for the majority of these children (78%) with only 7% of the children who denied moving directly to active disclosure. Active disclosure, operationally defined as a detailed, coherent, first-person account of the abuse, was eventually made by 96% of the children (including children who originally did not deny having been sexually abused). In approximately 22% of these cases, children recanted their allegations. Of those who recanted, 92% reaffirmed their allegations of abuse over time. The time frame involved in the progression through stages was unique to each case. Some children moved from denial to tentative to active disclosure in a single session; others took several months to reach the active phase. This study lends credibility to the intrapersonal-process model of children's disclosure of sexual abuse.

The intrapersonal-process model of disclosure of stigmatizing conditions has important practical applications. Health-care providers and significant others, such as sexual partners and parents, need to know that disclosure of stigmatizing conditions is not a dichotomous choice but an intrapersonal process that one goes through over a period of time. One's reaction to this disclosure is important in facilitating the intrapersonal process of disclosure of stigmatizing conditions. "When asked what the discloser wanted from respondents, they were clear that compassion, understanding, and information were most important" (Limandri, 1989, p. 76). Limandri (1989) states that "the responsiveness of the confidant is like a swinging gate permitting or preventing disclosure" (p. 76). Limandri (1989) goes on to argue that:

> disclosure does not imply that the person no longer feels stigma, but rather that the person feels less stigmatized. . . . In contrast, if a person disclosed in a guarded way and experienced rejection . . . , that person would probably feel greater stigma and would be less likely to disclose further. (p. 77)

In discussing the role of health-care providers, Limandri (1989) argues that health-care providers may facilitate or inhibit clients' disclosures:

> To provide relevant and necessary health care, providers must know the client's problem, and to do so requires the client disclosing that problem. Critical elements for facilitating disclosure . . . include developing a trusting relationship with the client and listening very carefully to cues that may be veiled disclosures. The nurse may facilitate disclosure by acknowledging cues and gently

exploring them by inquiring about specific possible stigmatizing
conditions. When the client denies any such conditions, the nurse
must remain open to the possibility while allowing the client to
retract temporarily. (p. 77)

The process model of children's disclosure of sexual abuse
also has practical applications for child-abuse detection by serving to increase professionals' understanding of the vacillating or
contradictory statements a child may offer regarding sexual
abuse. Instead of automatically assuming that denial of sexual
abuse means that abuse did not occur, professionals would
understand that this may be the first stage in the process of
disclosure of sexual abuse. Instead of viewing tentative statements or recanting of sexual abuse as indicating that a child is
lying, being coached, and so on, professionals would understand
that this behavior may be part of the intrapersonal process of
disclosure of sexual abuse. This model also offers valuable insight to the legal profession for interpreting the manner in which
children make disclosure of sexual abuse. The elements of negation, which are inherent in the intrapersonal process of children
disclosing sexual abuse, would no longer stand as a necessary
indictment against the veracity of the allegation.

Intrapersonal-process models of self-disclosure also can benefit general theory and research on self-disclosure. Intrapersonal-
process models of self-disclosure can be useful for extending
theoretical research on self-disclosure as a strategic behavior.
Miell studied the strategies people use to develop and restrict
the development of friendships (Miell, 1984; Miell & Duck,
1986). Miell found that self-disclosure was used strategically in
several ways, one of which was that individuals disclosed on a
topic in a relatively impersonal, or general, way and took note
of the partner's response to the general topic area before plung-
ing into a more detailed description (Miell, 1984). This allowed
them to predict a partner's likely response to their self-disclosure, thereby minimizing the risk of self-disclosure, before
engaging in self-disclosure. Similarly, Limandri (1989) states that
disclosure of stigmatizing conditions usually begins with "a

small revelation to test the environment" (p. 70). MacFarlane and Krebs (1986) state that "children frequently tell what happened to them in small pieces, saving the worst part until they see how their interviewer, their parents, or others react to the things they divulge first" (pp. 81-82).

Intrapersonal-process models of self-disclosure, specifically disclosure of family violence, also can be useful for extending the work of Petronio (1988), who examined privacy regulation as relationship specific. Petronio describes family members as both owners and caretakers of family information. Members are responsible for following the rules for disclosing family information, which differ from the rules for disclosing personal information. Petronio (1988) states that when violations do occur other members of the family issue punishment to the person responsible for disclosing the information. This perspective highlights a problem for individuals disclosing sexual abuse. Sexual abuse usually occurs within the family, and, therefore, exists as both personal and family information. The intrapersonal-process model of children's disclosure of sexual abuse could provide insight into the rules governing the regulation of information that belongs simultaneously to the individual and to the family.

Intrapersonal and Interpersonal Goals

That people have multiple, and often conflicting, goals in self-disclosure may serve as a useful center for synthesizing the act, intrapersonal-process, and interpersonal-process perspectives on self-disclosure. Self-disclosure serves functions consistent with each of these perspectives. Several approaches to the functions of self-disclosure have been elaborated (see Archer, 1987, for a review). Archer (1987) claims that these functions can be arranged from the most intrapersonal orientation to the most interpersonal orientation. In its most intrapersonally oriented form, self-disclosure functions as self-expression: It is used to express one's feelings. Self-disclosure also functions intrapersonally for self-clarification, to clarify one's feelings and beliefs, and for social validation, to find out where one stands in relation to others. Self-disclosure functions interpersonally as social control, or to obtain benefits or avoid punishments from others. Self-disclosure also is used interpersonally to elicit self-disclosure from others (reciprocity of self-disclosure). Finally, in its most interpersonal orientation, self-disclosure is used for relationship development, to represent and negotiate the relationship (Archer, 1987).

The act perspective focuses primarily on the intrapersonally oriented functions of self-disclosure: self-expression, self-clarification, and social validation. It is no wonder that from this perspective, self-disclosure is viewed as a uniformly positive act. The interpersonal-process perspective focuses primarily on the interpersonally oriented functions of self-disclosure: reciprocity of self-disclosure, self-disclosure and liking, and self-disclosure and relationship development. In traditional theories of relationship development, such as social-penetration theory, self-disclosure is viewed primarily as a positive act because self-disclosure is thought to be reciprocal, to induce liking, and to cause relationship development, although research on these topics indicates that there are major qualifications to all these claims. More recent dialectical approaches to relationship development explicitly argue that self-disclosure can have both positive and negative effects on a relationship. This is because people have multiple goals in self-disclosure and these goals may be conflicting. For example, the decision to disclose an affair to a spouse may involve the conflicting goals of self-expression and relational maintenance.

The goals of the intrapersonal perspective also are captured by the categories and functions of self-disclosure reviewed by Archer (1987). Nondisclosure (denial, tentative disclosure, and recanting of stigmatizing conditions) is individuals' attempts to shield themselves (and possibly their families) from negative evaluation and consequences, which are represented by the social control function. Active disclosure and reaffirming (after recanting) of stigmatizing conditions may involve self-expression, self-clarification, and self-validation. In addition, other factors may be involved: (a) More pragmatically in the case of family violence, active disclosure and reaffirming may reflect a desire to stop the abuse and to prevent the abuse of another, such as a sibling; and (b) in the case of AIDS, HIV infection, or herpes, active disclosure and reaffirming may reflect a desire to get medical attention, obtain social support, protect a sexual partner, or avoid losing a job, which are represented by the social control function.

The difficult part of self-disclosure is that, unlike the act perspective implies, individuals typically have multiple, and often opposing, goals when they self-disclose. If one's goals were solely to express one's feelings, then the consequences of self-disclosure might be uniformly positive. These goals, as suggested by the dialectical perspective, are often contradictory and produce dilemmas of both diagnosis and strategy (Rawlins, 1983).

Spitzberg (1993) also argues that the accomplishment of competent communication presents a variety of dialectical tensions, one of which is openness/intimacy versus closedness/autonomy. Spitzberg asserts that competence may be a more complex phenomenon than current conceptions and methods of communication competence suggest. Spitzberg (1993) argues "that competence possesses certain ideological components, and that it is likely to involve dialectical complexities that current conceptions have yet to resolve" (p. 140). Spitzberg (1993) goes on to argue that "If competence is an ability, then an actor must have the capacity to select from among tactical options those tactics that accommodate often opposing or incompatible goals" (p. 140).

The Intrapersonal-Interpersonal
Dialectical Perspective on Self-Disclosure

Although the intrapersonal and interpersonal perspectives on self-disclosure are identified and discussed separately in the literature, in truth, the intrapersonal process and the interpersonal process of self-disclosure interface to form an intrapersonal-interpersonal dialectical process of self-disclosure. As stated by

Altman (1993), "Inter-personal dialectical processes are probably often accompanied by intra-individual dialectics, with mutually influential effects occurring between them" (p. 28). Thus self-disclosure is a dialectical process that occurs both within and between persons. The intrapersonal-process perspective on the disclosure of stigmatizing conditions and children's disclosure of sexual abuse emphasizes the intrapersonal dynamics of self-disclosure; however, this perspective also implies interpersonal dynamics. Specifically, this perspective acknowledges that the process of self-disclosure is affected by a partner's response to self-disclosure (Limandri, 1989). Similarly, the dialectics of self-disclosure in relationships (Rawlins, 1983) is both an intrapersonal and an interpersonal phenomenon. Although relational dynamics are emphasized in this perspective, individual dynamics are implied. As aptly pointed out by Berger (1993) and by Altman (1993), the dialectical poles of openness and closedness are dealt with in the minds of individuals in a relationship (during and between their interactions) as well as between participants in a relationship (cf. Duck, 1980).

The perspective of self-disclosure as both an intrapersonal and an interpersonal dialectical process provides a more complete picture of the individual and relational dynamics of self-disclosure. The intrapersonal perspective highlights the process that individuals go through cognitively, whereas the interpersonal perspective highlights the process that relationships go through. The intrapersonal perspective highlights the cyclical nature of an individual's cognitions and behaviors, whereas the interpersonal perspective highlights the cyclical nature of relationships. Together these two perspectives provide the most insight into the skills of self-disclosure (and the skills involved in responding to self-disclosure). Although the skills (including diagnosis and strategy) of self-disclosure are far more complicated from this perspective, they also are more likely to result in effective communication than are skills portrayed from the act perspective, or from the intrapersonal or interpersonal perspective alone. The integration of the intrapersonal- and interpersonal-process perspectives on self-disclosure also holds promise for future theoretical and applied research on self-disclosure, and I urge those interested in the study of self-disclosure to pursue this line of thinking.

3

Transforming Relationships Through Ordinary Talk

Ted Spencer

It has long been held that relationship partners regulate their intimacy through the intimacy of their self-disclosures (Altman & Taylor, 1973). However, the Altman and Taylor (1973) social-penetration model has never established whether and how partners accomplish this through talk as it occurs in actual conversation; it simply holds intimate talk to be correlated with relational intimacy. Attempts to test theories of evolving intimacy through communication, such as social penetration or uncertainty reduction, have failed to demonstrate conclusively that specific patterns or elements of talk yield changes in relational intimacy (e.g., McKinney & Donaghy, 1993). Nevertheless, scholars continue to write about relationship communication as if these assumptions about talk and intimacy were well established. For example, Berg (1987) called disclosure reciprocity "by far the most consistent finding in the self-disclosure literature" (p. 111). But Dindia (1982, 1988) demonstrated that reciprocity research has relied entirely on correlational, self-report models, and her own sequential analysis of actual conversations revealed no evidence of self-disclosure reciprocity as an observable, measurable occurrence in actual conversation. My own study in parent-adolescent dyads (Spencer, 1993c) replicated Dindia's method, with the same findings. Our understanding of the dynamics of actual, ordinary relationship talk is clearly quite limited. This chapter therefore considers those limitations and then explores the ways in which ordinary talk affects various relational dynamics within the family and also within individual lives.

Research has been limited in the analysis of relationship communication in at least four ways that underestimate the role of ordinary talk in transforming individual identity and relationship dynamics: (a) an inaccurate and unsophisticated model of talk as a clear-channel conduit for information, (b) a focus on crisis or special-purpose talk, (c) a concern with individual utterances apart from the conversational sequences in which they are situated, and (d) a failure to examine the relational goals enacted by features of talk.

First, relationship research has been constrained by a model of talk that considers statements to be purely encoded and decoded representations of cognitions passed from one partner to another (cf. Duck et al., 1991); this model considers words to be accurate representations of a speaker's intentions and to be easily understood and interpreted by any listener with sufficient vocabulary. However, this model has been undercut by studies that show that participants' perceptions of a just-concluded get-acquainted conversation do not agree with regard to specific coding criteria (e.g., self-disclosure: Dindia, 1988; Reno & Kenny, 1992). The lack of intersubjective agreement suggests that something is different in the two persons' frames of reference about the conversation. In other work, Kreckel (1981) concluded that trained coders of conversation lack access to information used by family members in interpreting their own talk; family members demonstrated significantly higher agreement in segmenting family conversation and describing the functions of its component statements than did trained coders from outside the family. Kreckel's thesis holds that language within a related dyad (or subgroup) contains expressions and functions (a subcode to the common language code of the culture) that are embedded within the relationship, not just in the words of talk. To interpret accurately what is happening in family talk, we therefore need access to family-member perceptions. My own research (Spencer, 1993a) showed, however, that even with access to family-member perceptions there still can be poor levels of agreement in coding family conversation, particularly when coding for concepts derived from classic research (as I did with self-disclosure) instead of for concepts generated and identified by the speakers themselves (as Kreckel did). The problem with the "empty-conduit" model is that it fails to account for differences in speakers' frames of reference and their role in the shaping of meaning in talk. The words of the conversation are not the whole of the communication; they are a complex system of signs and symbols that participants use as one tool among many to negotiate meaning together.

A second limitation of relationship research is the use of crisis events or purposeful conversation as the sole source of relationship communication data. Duck et al. (1991) made use of the Iowa Communication Record to investigate the impact of various contextual aspects of daily talk on individuals and relationships. Duck (1994a, 1994b) argues that it is precisely the everyday talk patterns in a relationship, not just the crisis events, wherein a couple negotiates their relationship. However, current research (e.g., as presented in Kalbfleisch, 1993) makes too frequent use of written scenarios or hypothetical stimuli, to which participants are asked to give their response or to rate their perceptions of the people involved. To rise above this limitation, research must become interested in ordinary and natural exchanges of talk within relationships and look for relationship-changing dynamics there.

The third limitation of relationship research is the attention paid to isolated conversational utterances apart from the conversational sequences in which these utterances occur. Even coding methods such as Stiles's (1992) verbal response mode have been used more for quantifying proportional use of response modes rather than sequences. By contrast, Petronio (1991) examined the regulation of privacy boundaries in couples as they engaged in demand-response sequences that either invited or discouraged specific and intimate disclosures by the other in the conversation. In other words, ordinary talk sequences allow couples to define the level of intimacy for that particular part of the conversation and ultimately for the relationship as a whole.

The fourth limitation is that research into relationship talk is not always linked with a full investigation of relational goals that can be accomplished through talk. For example, self-disclosure typically is assumed to be linked with relational goals of developing intimacy, as in the social penetration model, but it is not often explored in relation to parental goals of modeling acceptable behavior (Spencer, 1993a). Reciprocity is considered (arguably) to be a feature of self-disclosure sequences, but its role in facilitating or hindering further disclosure has only recently been examined (Coupland, Coupland, Giles, & Wiemann, 1988). An exception to this critique is Tracy's (1991) volume on studies linking goals with discourse. This chapter therefore argues that ordinary talk is far more important to understanding relationships than previous research has assumed; that it carries relationship-changing dynamics between partners, such as regulating (rather than merely increasing) relational intimacy; and that, in particular, family members develop patterns of talk that are central to both family and individual developmental processes.

In fact, the family is a uniquely interesting arena for studying dynamics of "ordinary talk" (or "everyday talk," "natural discourse," "conversation") and its ongoing impact on developing relationships. Consider typical elements of a family, specifically the relationship between parent and older adolescent: They are closely related and involved (i.e., intimate) relationship partners; they have a long relationship past and presume a long relationship future; and they engage in regular interaction, typically involving talk. The long relationship past and future not only invoke issues of developmental change in the children's own cognitive and emotional growth, but the child's individual development implies relationship changes with parents as the child grows to adolescent and eventually to adult. Families, then, provide an ideal naturally occurring system in which relationship dynamics can be examined through ordinary talk.

Within the family, the relationship between parent and older adolescent highlights relational goals within the developmental process of individuation. This chapter therefore focuses on the adolescent-parent relationship; but in order to relate the study of family talk to the relational goals of parents and adolescents, a brief review of current adolescent individuation theory is needed.

Adolescent Individuation

Stage theories of adolescent development have long recognized adolescents' need to separate from their families. Recent theories of individuation suggest that multiple tasks are involved for the successful progression from dependent adolescent child to independent young adult. Grotevant and Cooper (1985, 1986) argue that individuation consists of two concepts: individuality and connectedness. Individuality is the ability to express separation from others as well as to assert personal views; connectedness includes the ability to display sensitivity, respect, and responsiveness to the ideas of others. Both concepts must be present for adolescents to take mature roles and form separate identities.

Smollar and Youniss (1989) identified a three-stage process of individuation, moving from (a) the perception of a need for autonomy, to (b) the stage of separation, to (c) seeing parents as persons, where the young adult develops a new intimacy with parents based on an equal-status relationship rather than a dependent-status relationship. Smollar and Youniss's interviews suggested that the third stage does not typically occur until young adulthood (i.e., over 20) if at all.

Ryan and Lynch (1989) demonstrated the importance of connectedness by finding a negative association between emotional autonomy from parents and measures of perceived lovability, family cohesion, and independence support. In other words, autonomy need not extend to emotional bonds for adolescents to develop a mature identity and independent role in the family.

In summary, adolescent individuation is marked by the adolescent's ability to make independent decisions and express personal views and goals to family members while maintaining positive emotional ties (or intimacy) with family members. What is still unclear, however, is the role of ordinary discourse in shaping relationships between parents and an adolescent, as the adolescent serves the goals of individuation.

Approaches for Studying Family Talk

There are several ways to approach the analysis of family talk that can help us to understand the relationship between dynamics of family interaction and positive outcomes of family growth and cohesion, adolescent development, and dyadic intimacy. These approaches use a variety of data sources, including interview data, self-report questionnaires, coding of discourse, and qualitative analysis of discourse. These approaches also consider family interaction from at least four perspectives: conversational frames of reference, topical issues of conversation, functions of discourse, and conversational sequences of interaction. Each perspective reveals a different impact of everyday talk on family relational processes.

Frames of Reference:
The Problem of Intersubjectivity

Kreckel (1981) found that family members share unique but overlapping frames of reference to such an extent that their natural discourse has a common subcode, a set of meanings that are known to that family in a way that may be misinterpreted by nonfamily members. She found that family members can segment and interpret their own discourse with more accuracy than trained nonfamily coders. Specifically, family members showed higher agreement in parsing their discourse into units and interpreting their functional meanings than nonfamily members did, even those with linguistic training. She also found that family members reached higher levels of agreement than outside coders when asked to label utterances according to their function in the conversation, a type of illocutionary coding. (The typology for coding was derived inductively from the family members' own labels.)

By contrast, my own study of self-disclosure between parents and adolescents (Spencer, 1993a) found that family members failed to reach strong levels of agreement in coding their conversational utterances as self-disclosure. Whereas Kreckel's (1981) findings would have predicted general agreement in this situation, studies by Dindia (1988) and by Reno and Kenny (1992) on self-disclosure between nonrelated acquaintances showed problems in attaining intersubjective agreement on the occurrence of self-disclosure in conversation; that is, Speaker A's self-report of self-disclosure in a just-completed interaction with Speaker B did not correlate significantly with B's assessment of A's self-disclosure. Dindia (1988) also failed to find significant correlations between the self-reports and objective coders' analysis of the audiotape data.

The issue is the extent to which we can predict intersubjectivity in family or intimate relationship talk. Do parent and adolescent truly share a language (or subcode) of conversation such that they understand each other's goals and experiences in conversation? Or do they speak past each other, uncertain or even ignorant whether their thoughts are being understood by the other? The problem of intersubjectivity highlights a too often ignored tenet of communication research, that conversational participants' frames of reference may not match; a listener may not understand an utterance in the same way the speaker intended.

The presence or lack of shared frames of reference has more than curiosity value to family functioning; the very forms of everyday talk used by a family are tools for solving problems with intersubjectivity. That is, when parent and adolescent discover that they are not in agreement when discussing "responsible behavior," they may talk through their disagreement until their frames of reference converge; perhaps they will redefine terms or establish common contexts. By contrast, another family may engage in talk that reinforces their individual positions and that does not seek common meaning.

It is possible then to consider the role that shared or disparate frames of references have on family talk and adolescent individuation. Perhaps we will find that adolescents and parents with closely shared values and goals maintain mutuality and connectedness better than adolescents and parents with conflicting values and goals. Or perhaps we will find that conflicting frames of reference in conversational interaction actually predict positive experiences of separation and autonomy. In either case, the intersubjectivity among family members has greatly underestimated importance in studying family talk. Until we study family talk using naturally generated talk (as opposed to staged, purpose-driven conversational tasks) together with the family members' interpretations of it, we will not be able to measure accurately intersubjectivity within conversation.

Information Control and Talk Topics

Asking subjects about their topics of conversation has long been of interest to self-disclosure researchers (e.g., Jourard & Lasakow, 1958); however, self-disclosure is not often discussed in relation to the functions of selecting or avoiding specific topics. Looking at conversational topics such as secrets (Vangelisti, 1994) or taboo topics (Baxter & Wilmot, 1985) within the family context is helpful to understanding family talk only when we can appreciate how the use or avoidance of a particular topic or content has a specific relational impact. How, for example, are individual goals and strategies facilitated by the use of one topic (such as college choices) and the avoidance of others (activities at a party)? In the one case, selecting or avoiding the topic of college choice can serve to protect or enhance the adolescent's autonomy from parents; selecting or avoiding the party topic may, in the other case, regulate the intimacy between them by exploring or avoiding intimate experiences.

What are the actual topics of conversation common between adolescents and parents, and how do they affect relationship dynamics? Vangelisti (1992) found that adolescents' conversational problems with parents were about topics related to individuation, particularly autonomy and separation. Typical problems were reported by adolescents to be centered around control of resources desired from parents, such as money or the use of the family car, or a request that parents cede responsibility and judgment to the adolescent, such as determining hours of curfew. The fact that adolescents consider these to be conversational problems suggests that they are actual topics of conversation with parents but not topics that are discussed with as much ease as, say, the results of the weekend football game or the last history test. It would be helpful to explore the features of this problematic talk in order to better understand the manner in which adolescents experience difficulty talking about status- and resource-related topics.

Avoiding talk about specific topics is a form of "information control" (Baxter & Wilmot, 1985). Controlled topics can come in the form of secrets or taboo topics, to name two. Avoidance of these topics has different impacts on relationship dynamics, depending on the type of avoidance.

Secrets

A secret is information that is intentionally concealed (Bok, 1983) from specific others; the information is seen to have value for those who possess it. According to Vangelisti (1994), secrets may be kept by individual family members, by coalitions within the family, or by entire families; secret topics often are related to stigma (Goffman, 1963) that could result from the secret being told. Keeping personal secrets from parents can have conflicting implications for a developing adolescent. On the one hand, information kept private can protect or enhance one's own status (Burgoon, 1982); the adolescent who does not talk about the prospective girlfriend/boyfriend with parents is keeping responsibility for decision making and guarding personal privacy.

On the other hand, keeping such matters private keeps the adolescent emotionally distant from parents by not inviting them to give support and encouragement; recall that emotional autonomy does not predict healthy separation/individuation (Quintana & Kerr, 1993). Keeping secrets within family coalitions also has implications for understanding adolescent individuation in the sense that individuation is measured within dyads, not as a personal achievement. In other words, a daughter may be highly individuated in her relationship with her mother, with whom she discusses many intimate details of her life, while remaining less individuated with her father, with whom she discusses far less.

Topic Referent

My research (Spencer, 1992) examined another content element of parent-adolescent conversation, the topic referent of a self-disclosure. If identified self-disclosures were rephrased into "I-statement" form (statements beginning with "I feel . . . ," "I think . . . ," "I did . . . ," "I want . . . "), who would be the object referent of the principal verb: the parent, the adolescent, their shared relationship, or some other third party? I found both adolescents and parents more likely to disclose their thoughts and feelings about the adolescent than about the parent. In other words, whereas adolescents disclose their own experiences, desires, and goals to parents, parents disclose their opinions about the adolescent's experiences, desires, or goals to adolescents. The imbalance could be explained either by a greater tendency among adolescents to exhibit conversational narcissism (Vangelisti, Knapp, & Daly, 1990) or, more likely, by a greater tendency among parents to display judgmental responses (which is what adolescents themselves believe parents do; Rawlins & Holl, 1988).

If in fact the parents are exercising control by maintaining the topics of conversation around the adolescents' experience as a method of judging and guiding their behavior, then we would expect adolescents with higher autonomy to avoid such control and to exhibit more balanced patterns, whereas adolescents in less individuated relationships would show less interest in hearing about their parents' life experiences than in discussing their own. Even if the imbalance is better explained by adolescent narcissism, Smollar and Youniss's (1989) final stage of individuation, "seeing parents as persons," would logically imply increasing curiosity about parents and less narcissism by the adolescent as the adolescent proceeds through individuation.

Time Frame: Processing of Experience

In the same study (Spencer, 1992), interview questions about topics of family self-disclosures revealed an interesting role played by time frames of conversation: Whether an event occurred in the past or present controlled many adolescents' decisions to disclose information to their parents. One daughter explained that she is more willing to talk honestly and openly about a difficult aspect of her relationship with her mother if approximately three months had passed since the experience that triggered the difficulty.

Although this daughter's processing of past experience happened privately, other families described processing experiences together through talk: Relationships developed and understanding increased as they repeatedly talked about past events. Processing allowed family members to understand each other's motives and perspectives better when their own needs were not as strong and their egos not as vulnerable. In exploring the content of conversational interaction, a distinction can be made between new information and old information; a troubling topic is first broached in the gentlest of terms, but as it recurs in later conversations it is discussed in greater precision and with more detail and less emotion. Eventually the topic has been repeated often enough that each participant is confident that the other will react with some predictable safety. The amount of new information in each iteration is kept manageable and nonthreatening.

This model of new-old information reiteration is especially suited to the family context in which members regularly encounter each other whether they are comfortable or not. Interviews (Spencer, 1993a) suggested three time orientations of self-disclosure:

1. Future talk disclosures. Expressions of hopes and goals or talk about anticipated events appear to be rare in family relationships except when concerning common rites of passage such as going to college or getting a car. They are generally optimistic rather than negative, although they may include negotiation of limits. Family members avoid conflict over future talk.

2. Present experience disclosures. These occur in several ways: *Idle chitchat* over schedules, activities, needs, and so forth is common, even though the feelings and desires underneath may be significant. Idle chitchat is a coordinating activity accomplishing family business. *Disagreements* may occur immediately at the time of trouble, although this is most likely when parent and adolescent are, for the present circumstances at least, acting as status equals. Regulations also may be disclosed for present events and concerns, given by the parent who is asserting an upper-status role.

3. After-event processing disclosures. Family members may choose to resolve differences at a time when tempers are steady and emotions are aligned or controlled. This may include revealing past problems unknown to the other partner, or it may mean resolving leftover feelings from a prior conflict. It also may include reminiscences, particularly when both family members are preparing for another turning-point experience such as leaving for college; it is common for relationship talk to emerge over the separation that was already in process.

In summary, several conversational topics have been identified as having the impact of regulating intimacy and autonomy within developing family relationships: secrets and privacy topics, topic referents, and time frames of talk, including after-event processing.

Functional Conversational Behaviors

Research has been much more active in studying adolescent communication in the family by studying the functions of particular statements made in family conversations. Grotevant and

Cooper (1985, 1986) coded utterances in family do-something-together tasks that presented a problem to solve and offered the fantasy of unlimited resources. Each transcribed utterance was classified into 1 of 14 behavioral indicator categories, such as "Agrees With/Incorporates Other's Ideas," "States Other's Feelings," or "Acknowledgment." The 14 indicators generated a weak four-factor solution of *self-assertion, permeability, mutuality,* and *separateness* as identifiable conversational behaviors related to individuation functions.

Problems arise in coding transcribed utterances by function; some commonplace utterances may have more than one possible meaning depending on context (Heritage, 1984), whereas phrases may have multiple functions (van Kleeck, Maxwell, & Gunter, 1985). Comprehensive coding systems are not well equipped to evaluate ambiguity and multifunctionality in family talk; systems that are designed to isolate a particular variable may have more success.

Hauser et al. (1984, 1987) isolated the *constraining* and *enabling* functions of speeches in family problem-solving discussions. Remarks that focus the conversation, solve problems, explain thoughts, or express curiosity were coded as "cognitive enabling," and speeches that devalue others or express indifference were "affective constraining." Fathers used cognitive-enabling speeches more often, particularly when addressing the adolescent directly. Mothers used more constraining speeches in general but not when addressing the adolescent directly.

The findings of Hauser et al. can be compared to teenagers' own perceptions that they receive more acceptance from peers and judgments from parents (Rawlins & Holl, 1988). Teenagers apparently are more aware of the constraining function of their parents' speech and the enabling function of their peers' speech. Closer study of conversational utterances is needed to help us understand what precisely constitutes enabling or constraining speech; research has not confirmed that family members themselves share the same perceptions as nonfamily coders on the functions of their natural talk. Nevertheless, the issue of relational constraint or enabling through speech is at the heart of this chapter's focus, and it is possible to look at conversational sequences for evidence of constraining or enabling conversational intimacy and self-disclosure.

Conversational Sequences

It is naive to study each utterance in a conversation as having its own impact on a listener that can be coded, measured, and interpreted apart from the surrounding sequence. A more sophisticated and accurate model portrays the unfolding conversational sequence as the carrier of interaction between speakers that allows speakers to have an effect on each other in order to accomplish relational goals. Several methods have been used to study conversational sequences: Ethnography of natural conversation and time-series analysis of conversational occurrences are two. In this section I present excerpts from parent-adolescent conversations together with interview data to illustrate how family conversational patterns can facilitate or hinder individuation in relationships. Further research can test these qualitative conclusions quantitatively and against appropriate measures of individuation.

For the sake of focus, let us look specifically at one conversational behavior within sequences, self-disclosure. The choice is made easier by the taxonomy ethnographically developed by Coupland et al. (1988) in studying sequences surrounding painful self-disclosure in intergenerational adult communication. Their sequences involved both precontext, the conversational context or stimulus for the self-disclosure, and recipient next-moves, the response given by the listener to the self-disclosure. Precontext can come from either speaker, from out of the blue, or from the textual flow of the conversation, whereas the recipient responses can range from those that encourage further disclosure to those that discourage it.

I report here on 24 conversations between high school juniors and seniors and one of their parents. The conversations were stimulated by a Turning Point Conversation Task (Spencer, 1993b) that invited participants to discuss for 10 minutes turning points in their family relationships over the past year. Participants reported their conversations as reflecting ordinary patterns of conversation. Even though the format was artificial, demands were minimal; the unequal status relationship of the dyads was left unaltered.

As the Coupland et al. (1988) taxonomy illustrates, there are two ways of looking at conversational sequence: forward and backward. Conversational precontext seeks to explain whether there was an important element earlier in a conversation that elicited the statement in question. In the family context, we are looking to see how self-disclosures in family dyads were brought about in sequence. By comparing the characteristics of the family relationships that use particular sequences, we can suggest some possible understandings about how these conversational sequences are attributes of individuated or unindividuated relationships.

Precontext

Direct Questions. Several parents engaged in direct elicitation of adolescent self-disclosures through the use of direct questions. One son reported self-disclosing more in the stimulated conversation than he reported was his habit in everyday interaction; the transcript reveals the father asking a series of direct questions of the son. The son therefore responded to the father's direct questions by disclosing the requested information.

In Dialogue 1, the father uses direct questions to elicit disclosures from the son, yet the son avoids responding directly. The father's questions differ from questions asked by less dominating parents in his use of limited-response-set questions. The father is requesting confession and agreement answers, such as "Yes, I understand, I'm sorry." The son tries to explain his perspective, but the father returns repeatedly to the question. These interrogation sequences are argumentative rather than cooperative.

Dialogue 1

Father: You do realize that what you did was wrong?

Son: Yeah.

F: I mean—He cheated you, and we knew all about that, and you were honest with that—with us about that. But, uh, you know that it's wrong to go up and physically hit somebody, especially somebody wearing glasses? I mean . . .

S: (laughing)

F: Well, I'm ju- just . . . I mean, do you recognize . . . ?

S: [You're] just partial to people who are wearing glasses.

F: Do you recognize the, why that was a bad thing to do?

S: Yeah. I mean, I was just mad because I knew—I knew he didn't get in trouble, and

F: Well, that—that wasn't our problem. That was his problem.

S: Well, I understand that.

F: And, uh, how do you know that he didn't get into any trouble?

S: I—I'm just sure he didn't.

F: You don't think his father was upset when he found out that he had tried to rip you off?

S: No, because his parents were so out of it that they thought, I'm sure they thought he didn't try.

F: Well, maybe so, but that isn't really—You know that isn't our problem. Our problem is that you started this fight, and, uh, could have hurt this kid, and it was a dangerous thing to do. It was a—You know it wasn't the kind of thing that, that I would expect you to do, you know, at your age. So I don't think the—that the fact that you were grounded for half of s-, uh, six weeks—what was it?—three weeks you were grounded? for starting a fight, where some kid has his glasses broken . . .

S: Yeah, but they weren't broken when I hit him. He broke them himself.

F: Well, maybe so, but still: What if you were—What if you had been in our shoes . . . ?

S: I ended up paying for the glasses.

F: What if you—Right, I know that—But what if you had been in our shoes? What would you think would have been a fair punishment?

S: Hmm. Well, I mean, I had to pay for the glasses, so that was punishment enough.

Individuation is limited in this dyad. The father does not offer his son autonomy; his desire to control is evident. The son actively maintains his own view but never receives acceptance of his viewpoint as valid. At least he receives an acknowledgment of a few of his opinions ("well, maybe so") without contradiction. The son is asking for more autonomy than his father is granting.

Nor is intimacy evident in the conversation; the entire 10 minutes of the stimulated conversation were spent on two topics where the son had been disciplined or where his judgment was disapproved. The lack of reciprocal patterns of talk (questions flowing in both directions, alternating from time to time) and the lack of affirmative responses to questions both would seem to indicate that the use of direct questions along the pattern shown in Dialogue 1 are signs of stifled individuation in the relationship.

Indirect Questions. A different pattern emerges in a dyad in which the mother indicates in her interview that her primary purpose in her conversations with her son is to let go, to encourage him to become his own person. She shows an interest in understanding her son's perspective, and she offers her perspective while attempting not to judge his views (Dialogue 2).

In this case, her first question to him is not direct; rather it opens the door for an answer: "I don't know if you felt that way." Although it is not stated in the form of a question, it functions as a question.

Dialogue 2

Mother: Uh, the other one I put down was—I put in September, when you told us that you didn't want to go to college, and that you really wanted to be a musician. And I mean, it freaked us out; but after we accepted that, and I, you know, felt like we supported you

Son: mm-hmm

M: in—in pursuing your dream, you seemed much happier and much more content

S: mm-hmm

M: just to be at home and to be around us. It's like we weren't the enemy anymore. I don't know if you felt that way . . .

S: No, I—

M: That's the way I perceived it, is that all of a sudden we weren't the bad guys anymore, and that you could be yourself around here and say anything you wanted to.

S: That's pretty much it. 'Cause I felt bad when Dad said that he felt he had failed as a parent because I didn't want to go to college, 'cause I thought that was ridiculous. Because going . . .

M: Well . . .

S: Well, going, I mean, going to college is not—Being a good parent is not making your kid go to college if that's not what he wants.

M: But you've got to understand that that's what Dad had drummed into his brain.

S: Yeah, I understand that.

M: For years, I mean, [his mother and father] taught those kids that education is more important than anything.

S: Well, and I agree that education is important.

M: Oh, sure. [not sarcastic]

S: But, I mean, that's my—I mean honestly, I mean—I know we've discussed this, we don't have to get into it; but I mean, if—You know as well as I do, that if I turn 35 and I didn't give the music a chance, I'd never be able to forgive myself.

Indirect questions can be a sign of offered autonomy. The extent to which they are accepted and responded to by the adolescent may indicate the degree to which the adolescent seeks and expresses autonomy.

Modeling. A function of self-disclosure not commonly described in research, but mentioned in several interviews, is the parent's self-disclosure as a model for the adolescent. By stating what she feels about a given topic, a mother can let her daughter know that the daughter may feel free to discuss the topic along similar lines without fear of an uncomfortable response from the mother. It is a preemptive self-disclosure; it establishes the safety of a topic.

The nature of self-disclosure as modeling behavior contributes to a view of everyday conversation as evolving meaning (Duck et al., 1991). One of the difficulties in coding self-disclosure by family members (Spencer, 1993a) is in identifying the revelatory aspect of a disclosure (Jourard & Lasakow, 1958). Interviews revealed that conversational topics recur over time with ever-increasing detail, indicating that as time passes, participants are more able to discuss a topic in intimate detail. One of the apparent purposes of repetitive and evolving self-expression is to estab-lish the safety of the territory in which self-disclosure is to take place. As an adolescent gains insight into the parent's probable response, for example, the adolescent can decide whether it is "safe" to self-disclose. Parents can accomplish the same thing, but rather than hinting around a topic to discover the adolescent's typical responses, the parent expresses an opinion around a topic she or he hopes to hear the adolescent discuss so as to preempt the need for hinting by the adolescent.

In this case, the use of modeled self-disclosures may be more a sign of offered intimacy by the parent than of offered autonomy. A modeled self-disclosure would seem likely when the topic is potentially more intimate than the relationship could stand, according to the modeling discloser's perspective. To the extent that the recipient responds with a matched self-disclosure, the recipient can be seen to accept the offered advance in intimacy. Although modeling was mentioned only by parents in inter-views, it is reasonable to expect that adolescents are equally capable of setting the stage for intimacy through modeled self-disclosures.

Need for Attribution. "It just needed to be said," was a typical answer to the interview question, "Why did you self-disclose at this point?" and illustrates Coupland et al.'s (1988) categories that refer to a need for an attribution to explain a potential mis-understanding. Using both the Coupland et al. (1988) coding and lag sequential analysis, I (Spencer, 1993c) found that parents and adolescents tend to disclose out of a proactive position rather than a reactive one; it was not common for speakers to wait to be invited in order for them to proceed with a self-disclosure. Rather, speakers often found the need or desire to explain their meaning as way to establish a reputation with the other.

For example, one daughter had begun taking birth-control pills for medical reasons. Her mother several times offered her understanding and willingness to discuss the topic of birth control and sexuality, but the daughter emphatically repeated, "It's not for birth control, Mom," adding that she wants to make sure her mother understands that.

Another daughter showed a high degree of conflict with her family on the screening instrument for participation, but she insisted to the attending clinician that she wanted to participate in the research task. Her conversation (Dialogue 3) showed several examples of assertive self-disclosures.

Dialogue 3

Mother: But you wanna—Do you want to talk about when [ex-husband/stepfather] left and stayed gone for three days and didn't call?

Daughter: I just don't think you should have taken him back after that, because, you know, whenever I left that one time, and, you know, you weren't going to take me back? But you were able to, but you took him back?

M: Well, um, I think basically what that was, was that you weren't, um, willing to communicate, and you weren't willing to cr—, uh, to meet me—At least, the way I felt, I felt like you were not trying to work things out, and you were not willing to follow direct—follow uh rules—or, or the things that I expected of you, you weren't willing to do them. And that's why I asked you, I mean that's why I told you that unless you could follow the rules, then, um, you can come home. Because you left the house, you were going to be— um—I'm willing to work it out [inaudible] in order to stay gone.

D: That's what I was trying to do.

M: I just told you you needed to stay gone.

D: That's what I was trying to do. I was trying to talk to you on the phone before I came home.

M: Because you didn't want to be grounded.

D: Because—No, it wasn't that. You never even asked me why. The reason why I didn't want to come home until we had talked about it was because I didn't want to come home and for it to be the way it was when I did come home. When I came home you wouldn't talk to me.

The emphatic use of attributions for clarification functions as a demand for autonomy by the daughter. The need for clarification is exacerbated by the parent's own use of attribution in place of a less combative response; had the mother inquired further about the daughter's reasons, or responded in an empathic, neutral, or even reciprocal way to the daughter's previous explanation, the exchange would have functioned more to negotiate together the adolescent's autonomy rather than for the adolescent to seize it.

Summary. Conversational sequences, here centering around self-disclosures, reveal patterns that vary from parent assertive, in which parents ask questions and in which parents or adolescents state their opinions and judgments uninvited by the other, to mutually responsive, in which parents and adolescents exchange insights through coordinated self-disclosures and modeling disclosures. As adolescents assert their own autonomy in their family relationships, parents have the option of battling the adolescent to retain their own assertive dominance in the relationship, as shown by the father in Dialogue 1 and the mother in Dialogue 3, or parents can become responsive to the adolescent's concerns in a way that facilitates exchange of disclosure, as shown in Dialogue 2.

It is also interesting to note, in the two combative conversations shown above in which autonomy is desired by the adolescent but not freely offered by the parent, that intimacy appears to be relatively lacking in the interaction. Quintana's research showed that healthy individuation does not arise from separation and connectedness alone but also from positive experiences of each. There are maladaptive ways of separating and maladaptive forms of attachment. Quintana and Kerr (1993) summarized separation/individuation research as suggesting "that college students benefit from (a) secure attachment to parents in which there is mutual trust, communication, and little conflict or alienation and (b) relationships with parents in which their separateness and individuality are mirrored, acknowledged, and supported" (p. 349). It is reasonable to conclude that where parents attempt to manipulate their adolescents' responses and do not offer encouragement to speak freely, the development of intimacy in individuation will be delayed.

This is in fact the dilemma faced by gay and lesbian adolescents/young adults who want to come out to parents but whose parents are not willing to grant them respect for their declaration. These sons and daughters must choose between maintaining intimacy with their parents and sacrificing their personal identities within the family, or they must sacrifice the past level of intimacy in favor of taking the autonomy they need to maintain their identity as sexual persons (Spencer, 1991).

Recipient Next-Moves

How a listener responds to a speaker's statement (again in this context, self-disclosures) is equally useful in understanding the relational impact of everyday conversation in a family. But here, rather than looking backward to see what elicits a statement, we look forward to see how a statement was received by examining the response given.

No Response/Minimal Response. Nonresponse patterns can be ritualized or natural. Two families described ritualized (weekly) family meetings in which each family member takes a turn talking without interruption. The ritualized nonresponse pattern was most evident in one particular dyad whose 10-minute conversation had only 22 speaker-turn segments throughout.

The other nonresponse pattern was not ritualized; it consisted mainly of fathers who used minimal responses such as "mm-hmm" to leave the floor to the adolescent. As one father admitted, he withheld his comments until he was confident that his son had expressed himself as much as he cared to on the topic.

The nonresponse pattern represents a system that fosters independence and autonomy in each family member. The frequency of the interaction may be a factor enhancing the development of conversational intimacy.

Perspective-Changing Responses. The nonresponse and minimal-response patterns can be considered accepting and encouraging responses because they neither contradict the discloser nor upset the rhythm of the discloser's speaking turn. Even when the speaker completes a phrase and the recipient has the opportunity to speak, the recipient can refuse the opportunity, as in the above-described patterns. But coding of next-moves (Spencer, 1992) showed that a disproportionate number of response patterns are in the category of adding context to the disclosure, with the minimal moves of "uh-huh" and "mm-hmm" next on the list. The "adding-context" category includes both argumentative contradictions, opinions, and judgments, as well as cooperative elaborations and statements of approval or agreement. Both father and son in Dialogue 1 show the contradictory patterns of responses; the mother and son in Dialogue 2 show cooperative patterns. It would be hasty to conclude, then, that the recipient next-move category of "adding context" is truly only discouraging of self-disclosure; it appears that adding context also can serve an encouraging role.

Rhythmic Changers. Finally, two response devices are used by some speakers to alter the common rhythm of disclosure-response. Participants remarked in interviews how often interruption occurred in their audiotapes; both father and son in one dyad noticed that the father interrupted the son often, taking the floor when it was not yielded. Other participants used spacers, responses that were nonresponsive to a first request for disclosure, but that were followed a turn later by a more appropriate response. By distancing themselves from the direct question with a non-response, recipients are able to assert more independence and less responsiveness in interaction.

Dialogue 4

Mother: But, you know, I have—I have noticed that, um, you—you do care about what I say. I mean, before in your adolescence or your teenage, you blew me off as someone who didn't know what she was talking about. But you—you show me a lot of respect, something that the other boys don't do yet; and you hadn't just until recently. You do care! I mean, you can say you don't—

Son: I was tapping my pen—I was scratching it. [N.B.—apologizing about interfering with tape recording]

M: Do you feel like you do care about what I say? Or am I just imagining it?

S: I have been a lot more than I used to.

M: It's like, you'll do what it takes to make me happy without me telling you—like you really care about what makes me happy.

S: Well, then why do you come into my room sometimes and say, "You don't care about me. You don't do anything to show that—that you're thanking me for anything!" [mock serious tone]

M: [laughs] That's because of what I'm going through physically. I do that with all of—everybody. That's a whole 'nother story. That's—But I do no- I notice that you do care. I notice that a lot.

S: Well—I noticed you care too, Mom. I really have.

M: [laughs] Oooohh! [sentimental sigh]

S: For real! You called the lifeguard thing for me—that was pretty nice.

M: Well, I want you to have all the advantages you can. I know that with your school, and your workin', you don't have the opportunity to call all these people. So—

S: Yeah.

M: Sometimes I feel like I'm interfering.

S: No, you're not.

Petronio (1991) theorized that relational partners regulated the degree of privacy in their conversation by negotiating the specificity to be used in question-answer sequences. That is to say, if one partner asked a general, ambiguously phrased question, the other partner was free to remain noncommittal and vague in response, thereby preserving some relational distance and privacy over the topic. The use of spacers in Dialogue 4 serves the similar purpose of regulating the level of intimacy and amount of detail to be used in exchanging conversational self-disclosures. In this case, the mother asks a question that presumes a certain level of intimacy in the conversation. She, in fact, makes clear that she expects an intimate response about how much her son cares for her; it is a high-certainty demand. He spaces the question with an irrelevant comment to indicate his refusal of her demand for a private disclosure; it is a low-certainty response. After she repeats the demand, making clear that she wants a response, he expresses the information that he felt was keeping him from expressing complete agreement, a high-certainty response. Once she has accepted his negative disclosure, he is willing to continue forward with an intimate response. In fact, his first response after her explanation is a low-certainty response, merely restating the initial question in affirmative form. As she then responds likewise with a low-certainty response, he comes back with a higher certainty explanation to reinforce her perception and to show that he is genuinely appreciative, not just giving the requested response.

Both speakers play a role in establishing the level of intimacy to be shared in conversation; as the degree of certainty in the demand (high) matches the degree of certainty in the response (low, then high), the dyad can coordinate privacy boundaries and maintain comfort and intimacy in the relationship. If a high-certainty demand is met by a low-certainty response, the request for intimacy through sharing across privacy boundaries is denied, leading either to stasis or to relationship withdrawal.

Summary. Nonresponse, minimal response, context-changing responses, and spacers are examples of the impact that one's responses can have on encouraging the other's conversation (and by implication, their points of view) or challenging the other's judgments as somehow improper, insufficient, or unappreciated. As parents encourage adolescents in their talk, allowing them to explore their own points of view, the parents are encouraging the assertion of separation and autonomy from parental views. As adolescents show signs of encouraging parents in their own disclosures, they are displaying a curiosity and interest in knowing parents as persons in their own right, a sign of developing relational intimacy.

Longer Conversational Sequences

Earlier reference was made to interview material that suggested longer time-frame sequences of conversational interaction within families than are available for study within single conversational occurrences. For example, the point was argued that family members discuss topics repetitively over time, each time disclosing at some more explicit level of detail or making more clear their particular intentions and desires with regard to the topic.

Another way to look at longer conversational sequences, however, is to look at ongoing conversational patterns within a family over time. The most intriguing personal discovery in my research (Spencer, 1992) was to notice a pattern in several dyads that can only be labeled a long-term conversational strategy, one that seemed to correspond with some highly individuated relationships. Some parents displayed a blend of curiosity and empathy toward their adolescent that showed up both in the interview and in their conversational style. These parents were genuinely interested in learning what their adolescents were thinking and feeling and were willing to set aside their own prejudgments long enough to listen to the adolescent's explanations and attributions; these were the parents who were most likely to elicit frequent and intimate self-disclosures from their adolescents. The parents who offered multiple perspectives on the adolescent's disclosure topic without contradicting the adolescent's own perspective were also the parents who encouraged conversational self-disclosure to continue free-flowing.

Note that the above observation is one-sided in favor of the parent's influence on the adolescent's disclosure; I was more aware of the parent's impact on their family conversation patterns than I was of the adolescent's impact. The exception was in the families who reported high amounts of conflict; in these conversations it was common to see the adolescent using more frequent topic shifts or switches and being nonresponsive to direct questions, thereby preventing intimacy from occurring through coordinated disclosures and responses.

Summary

This chapter has dealt with features of everyday, ordinary talk that serve to regulate intimacy, status, privacy, or identity between relational partners, specifically using examples from parent-adolescent relationships. It has argued that relationship research has much more to learn about the manner in which relationship partners engage in everyday talk, and that such research should seek to explain the impact that ordinary talk has on relationship dynamics.

In contrast to past approaches of coding individual statements according to function, this chapter has looked at conversation as multitextured and sequential, with the perceptions of partici-

pants (i.e., their own codings) being vital to an accurate interpretation of statement functions and the sequential context required to interpret the intent and the response of conversational
partners. It is important to emphasize that family systems are
but one context in which the relationship dynamics presented
here are transacted through ordinary talk, and the dynamics of
intimacy, autonomy, identity, and status are but a few of the
processes that are of interest to relationship researchers.

Dispelling Doubt and Uncertainty:
Trust in Romantic Relationships

Susan D. Boon

In a recent depiction of the state of
personal relationships research, Duck
(1994b) raised the compelling argu-
ment that our research inquiries have as yet tended to neglect
an entire realm of relationship phenomenon: the darker side of
relationships or unpleasant nether regions which talk show
hosts find so appealing yet which remain virtually untouched
by scientists. In our haste to open to empirical observation the
uncharted topography of intimacy and closeness, for example,
we have left unexplored vast tracts of relationship terrain, including such experiences as unrequited love, betrayal, and obsession.
Although less positive in aspect, these unmapped domains are
also of substantial importance in understanding interpersonal
relations and worthy in their own right of researchers' attention.

To which side of the relationship fence, if any, does a discussion of interpersonal trust belong? In my view the answer to this
question is more complicated than one might initially think. On
the one hand, healthy, satisfying relationships are thought to be
characterized by mutual trust between partners. Relationships

in which pockets of distrust and doubt remain unresolved do not measure up to our ideal standards for a good relationship.

On the other hand, in coming to a full understanding of the nature of trust in interpersonal relationships, I believe we also must consider the appreciable risk inherent in the act of trusting a partner, the vulnerable stance we adopt when we place our faith in a partner's benevolent intentions. Indeed, as I endeavor to argue throughout this chapter, it is possible and perhaps advantageous to construe the process of trusting a partner as an act of risk taking.

I will certainly not be the first to assert the claim that a decision to trust typically involves considerable risk and is made under appreciable uncertainty (Boon & Holmes, 1991; Holmes, 1991; Kelley & Thibaut, 1978; Kelvin, 1977; Lewis & Weigert, 1985a, 1985b; Luhmann, 1988; Silver, 1989; Thomas, 1978). The very nature of situations in which trust is required demands that trust be an optimistic forecast of things to come, rather than a factually based certainty. Indeed, theorists have argued cogently that "trust begins where knowledge ends" (Lewis & Weigert, 1985a, p. 462) and, moreover, that trust is possible only where opportunities for experiencing risk and vulnerability exist (Holmes, 1991; Kelley & Thibaut, 1978; Luhmann, 1988; Silver, 1989). Accordingly, a discussion of the dynamics of trust leads us necessarily into a consideration of this darker realm of relationship experience, to those relatively uncharted regions where people are not always nice to each other and the prospects of pain and betrayal often loom large on the horizon.

Trust as Risk Taking: Toward a Definition

Just as a pair of mountain climbers must coordinate their movements in order to maintain their precarious grip and keep from plummeting to the hard ground below, so, too, becoming intimately involved with another is a venture in which two individuals strive to reconcile their needs, goals, and desires and to maintain the delicate balance required to preserve the relationship intact. Extending the analogy further, as time passes and a relationship expands in depth and breadth of involvement—as the climbers ascend higher and higher on the mountain wall—the elements of risk associated with depending on another actually increase. First, the level of interdependence is intensified and, in correspondence, the stakes to be lost rise substantially. Furthermore, it becomes increasingly apparent that the efforts of neither partner alone can achieve the balance required to maintain the relationship. A solo climber is a foolish climber, and if either partner loses his or her grip, both may plunge headlong to the valley floor beneath.

This analogy highlights a number of elements important to understanding the interface between trust and risk. Every day in our relationships we must make decisions: decisions to commit further or to withdraw, to take this course of action in response to a situation of conflict versus some alternative action, to make use of a particular opportunity or to let it pass us by. Often these decisions are difficult and risk laden, compelling us to confront our hopes and fears about depending on another for our own needs to be met. In the same very real way that mutual trust enables a pair of mountain climbers to conquer the mountain, it provides the critical platform from which relationship partners may confidently approach the task of decision making. It provides the implicit contract of good intentions that permits the negotiation of situations that conspire to awaken us to the ways in which we are vulnerable in our relationships.

Kelvin (1977) argues that people use attitudes, expectations, and the like to impose order on a world that otherwise often would appear capricious and unpredictable. Consistent with this logic, I define interpersonal trust as the confident expectation that a partner is intrinsically motivated to take one's own best interests into account when acting—even when incentives might tempt him or her to do otherwise (see also Boon & Holmes, 1991). According to this working definition, a sense of trust is essentially an optimistic outlook regarding the likely consequences of depending on another in situations of risk, an outlook that permits doubt and feelings of vulnerability to be supplanted by a sense of assurance and feelings of security. Mutual trust exists when both partners in a relationship share such positive convictions about each other's motives and intentions.

Although trust is an important component of any interaction in which the participants are interdependent, the dynamics peculiar to romantic relationships provide a canvas against which the processes involved in the growth, maintenance, and decay of trust may be painted in vivid detail. Our popular culture and folk wisdom are replete with testaments to the risk, the pain, and the potential for loss characteristic of becoming close to and depending on romantic partners. In the sections that follow I articulate in detail the nature of interpersonal trust as it operates within romantic relationships, charting its course throughout the transition from early contact to established relationship and afterward.

A Portrait of Trust in Romantic Relationships

Unfurling the Pathway to Mutual Trust

Developmental theorists have long held that experiences in early childhood provide the point of departure for the development of capacities to place our faith and our trust in others (e.g., Ainsworth, Blehar, Waters, & Wall, 1978; Bowlby, 1973; Bretherton, 1990; Erikson, 1968; Main, Kaplan, & Cassidy, 1985; see also Beinstein Miller, 1993), claiming that patterns of responsiveness experienced in relationships with caregivers during our earliest years form the initial basis for expectations regarding others' willingness and ability to attend to our needs. Such expectations are believed to be the seeds from which later grow our ability to feel comfortable and secure becoming close to and relying on others.

According to attachment theorists such expectations are embodied in internal working models of self and other, dynamic representations of the attachment relationship that serve a variety of purposes in organizing attachment-related information (e.g.,

Bretherton, 1990; Main et al., 1985). Importantly, such working models also may lie at the foundational core of the process of appraisal (see Holmes, 1991) by which we assess information relevant to judgments regarding another's trustworthiness and the degree of risk associated with a trusting move in a given situation. In accord with this notion, a flurry of recent investigations of adult romantic relationships suggest that issues surrounding attachment—and their mental representation—may figure prominently in the dynamics of adult as well as childhood relationships (e.g., Hazan & Shaver, 1987; Kobak & Hazan, 1991). More to the point, several studies document evidence that adult attachment style is related to reported level of interpersonal trust among romantic partners (Boon & Holmes, 1990; Collins & Read, 1990; Simpson, 1990) as well as to general beliefs about the secure versus risky nature of dating relationships (Boon, 1992).

Although the true extent of continuity of such dispositional bases of trust remains an empirical question (see Bartholomew, 1993), it seems likely that chronic distrust born of rejection and/or inconsistent treatment in childhood may form an appreciable stumbling block in the path toward developing intimate and satisfying relationships with others throughout adolescence and adulthood. The appraisal process is not, however, an exclusive function of chronic expectations. Social psychological treatments of trust suggest that more acute situational factors also may play an important role in augmenting or attenuating an individual's willingness to trust a close other (e.g., Deutsch, 1958; Kelley & Stahelski, 1970; Strickland, 1958; Swinth, 1967). If the general implications of findings in this area of research may be applied to a consideration of trust in the domain of interactions among intimates, establishing the degree of risk inherent in any situation may be integral to understanding how and when people make decisions about whether or not to trust another on whom they are interdependent. When the structure of a situation conspires to raise the specter of being exploited or double-crossed if a person chooses to adopt a trusting course of action, the decision to trust is likely to pose a considerable dilemma.

Moreover, the ebb and flow of experiences that compose a relationship's history or interactional background provide the unique context within which decisions to adopt a trusting course of action are embedded, determining the flavor and function of trust within the specific relationship. A couple's shared experiences, including the successes and failures of their efforts at coordinating their needs when conflicts arise, serve to define the extent to which the partners are interdependent in the various spheres of their lives and, consequently, the relevance of trust for managing feelings of vulnerability evoked by situations of risk (Boon & Holmes, 1991; Holmes, 1991).

In this section I consider the growth of trust as it reflects the appraisal process and the changing concerns and issues that dominate partners' interests as their relationship progresses. From her analysis of the metaphors people use to describe their romantic relationships, Baxter (1992) concluded that "relationships may be characterized by transitory goals which are ever changing in response to ongoing discoveries the parties make about themselves, one another and their relationship" (p. 270). Such shifting goals and concerns guide my discussion of the development of trust, marking the pathway to a mutually felt confidence in the relationship.

The Romantic Love Stage

During the earliest stages of relationship growth, trust may be little more than a fragile expression of hope founded on an idealization of the partner and bolstered by denial of any fears and doubts concerning the lack of hard evidence to substantiate the optimistic forecast (Holmes, 1991). Amidst the profusion of positive feelings and experiences characteristic of this period, little significance is attached to an actual evaluation of the partner's motives; rather, a process of projection both fuels and protects an image of the partner as caring and benevolently motivated. It is no surprise, then, that trust and feelings of love tend to be closely linked at this time.

Although emotional involvement is typically intense during this stage of development, it is also rather superficial (Braiker & Kelley, 1979; Brickman, 1987; Eidelson, 1980). The arena for "interaction" is tightly constrained early in a relationship as partners attempt to ensure that their best selves are put forward. In addition, the partners' focus is on the rewarding qualities of the relationship, the things that make it seem worthwhile (Eidelson, 1980; Rusbult, 1983), rather than on an accurate evaluation of its future prospects. As a consequence, a person's expectations about a partner during this stage are little more than tentative theories that speculate, in the absence of real data, that the partner's feelings and motives are essentially equivalent to his or her own. The partner's attentions and affectionate overtures lend apparent support to these speculations, justifying the sense of optimism about the relationship's future.

Unless a sizable imbalance exists in the partners' involvement, however, any indications of caring are taken as evidence to corroborate the budding positive expectations about the partner. Only if the appraisal process exposes a considerable disparity in emotional investment is it likely that a person would even begin to question his or her optimistic assumptions about the partner (cf. Baier, 1986).

The Evaluative Stage

It is inevitable that this glow eventually fades, however, to be replaced by a somewhat more realistic view of the relationship in which the sometimes harsh light of reality slowly begins to intrude on the idealizations of the romantic love stage. As interactions become less regulated by impression-management concerns and the depth and breadth of interdependence in the relationship increase, the degree of fit between the partner and a person's romantic ideal often begins to break down. A new agenda emerges within the relationship as such imperfections gradually are revealed, with the ultimate goal being the reduction of the uncertainty that the new vision of the partner has thrust on the scene (Holmes, 1991; Kelvin, 1977). It becomes important at this juncture to establish in more objective terms the true worth of the partner, taking into consideration the implications of any negative aspects that might be detected (Brickman, 1987).

At this stage of relationship development it is often the case that certain unavoidable and somewhat unpleasant facts first become apparent. With reality casting shadows of doubt on the former optimistic assumptions regarding the partner's feelings and motives in the relationship, a person comes to realize that the continued growth of the relationship is likely to entail some degree of sacrifice, compromise, and accommodation (Kelley, 1983). Accordingly, this period is characterized by an emerging interest in evaluating the partner and the prospects for the relationship's future (Brickman, 1987; Eidelson, 1980; Holmes, 1991). Consequently, a more data-based appraisal strategy is implemented, with a focus on establishing relatively stable, unified expectations about the partner that might permit more accurate predictions about what the future of the relationship holds in store (e.g., Kelvin, 1977; La Gaipa, 1987). There is risk involved in this more evaluative stance, however: In some cases partners may be confronted by the unpleasant possibility that their relationship may ultimately fail.

Whereas the appraisal process within the romantic love stage focused attention rather exclusively on the rewards and benefits to be accrued within the relationship, during the evaluative stage the emphasis shifts to the symbolic meaning of a partner's overall pattern of behavior (Holmes, 1991; Kelvin, 1977). Behavior is monitored for evidence diagnostic of a partner's underlying motives and intentions, particularly with respect to the extent to which it signals emotional attachment and responsiveness (Reis & Shaver, 1988). The key issue of debate is whether such behavior is intrinsically as opposed to selfishly motivated: What's in it for the partner? The level of analysis thus becomes more abstract as the relationship progresses: Concrete rewards per se recede in importance at this stage in comparison to the symbolic messages conveyed by behavior, information that might support the belief that the partner is truly and unselfishly caring.

Counterintuitively, the newly awakened sense of vulnerability and uncertainty that accompanies discovery of the partner's "inadequacies" may in fact serve to augment opportunities for drawing charitable inferences about his or her motives and intentions (Kelley, 1979; Luhmann, 1988; Strickland, 1958; Swinth, 1967; Thomas, 1978). For example, Kelley and Thibaut (1978) claim that evidence about personal dispositions can be conclusive only when opportunities for betrayal or exploitation exist—when competing motives battle to control a partner's actions. Only then can intrinsic motivation be imputed when the partner overcomes the temptation and chooses instead to renounce his or her own preferences (see also Thomas, 1978). Congruent with this reasoning, Silver (1989) argues that trust acquires its meaning by virtue of the fact that the trusted other may at any time choose to act in a manner contrary to one's own best interests.

Thus as a relationship enters this period of evaluation the first real opportunities arise for an actual empirically based sense of trust to take root. Current levels of trust based on a perceived equivalence in emotional attachment and involvement (Boon & Holmes, 1991) set the pace of growth for this seed of trust, providing a base from which it is safe to initiate moves to increase intimacy and dependence, moves that reveal a person's intrinsic motivation in the relationship and set the stage for the next step in the development of a capacity to trust.

Once begun, the growth of trust is a conjunctive process (Holmes, 1991; Lewis & Weigert, 1985a), an emergent property of the relationship itself forged by the partners' joint endeavors (Acitelli & Duck, 1987; Kelvin, 1977; Reis & Shaver, 1988). The process involves an upward-spiralling series of mutually reciprocal and reassuring moves wherein partners successively increase their involvement and thereby express their love for each other and confidence in the value and security of the relationship. It is necessary that, at each step of this cycle, partners go beyond merely validating each other's former advance; the process of reciprocation must involve escalating responses if the proper balance of trusting overtures is to be attained. In fact, problems may result if either partner is too stingy or, conversely, too generous in his or her response at any level (Holmes, 1991; Rubin, 1974).

Typically, patterns of social exchange are examined within a relatively narrow time frame during this stage of development. The accounting process tracks the balance of give and take over a fairly short span of time, and evidence of reciprocity is evaluated in the short rather than the long term (Holmes, 1991). If, however, an accumulation of evidence points toward a partner's motives as consistently unselfish and intrinsic in nature, the consequent growth in mutual trust and attachment eventually may allow the partners to cast aside their feelings of vulnerability and insecurity and relinquish their concerns about ensuring that their own needs are met. Ideally, as the growing sense of trust continues to mature, the emphasis in accounting will shift from a concern with maximizing one's own outcomes to establishing the communal welfare of the couple as a whole (Murstein & MacDonald, 1983).

The Accommodation Stage

As the evaluative phase draws to a close, the stage is set for a period of accommodation in which the partners must seek mutually acceptable solutions to arenas of incompatibility and opposing interests exposed during the preceding period of evaluation. In many cases the restrictive costs of increased closeness and interdependence have begun to sting at this point, ambivalence and conflict are on the rise, and newfound incompatibilities among partners may seem poised to threaten the relationship's very existence (Eidelson, 1980; Kelley, 1983). In the heat of this field of combat a burgeoning sense of trust meets its final testing ground. This period of accommodation provides an opportunity for growth through conflict (Braiker & Kelley, 1979); by developing their own unique solutions to the dilemmas they face, a couple gains assurance that together they can effectively manage areas of conflict and disagreement in their relationship. Importantly, such assurance fuels feelings of security in the relationship, freeing the couple to relax their efforts at control and caution in other encounters with situations entailing potential risk (Holmes, 1991).

Some couples are unable to meet the demands of this accommodation process, unable to surmount the challenges they face in coordinating their needs and preferences. Perhaps they are too uncomfortable discussing conflictual issues openly; perhaps their differences are irreconcilable; perhaps their problem-solving efforts deteriorate into destructive shouting matches or ineffectual episodes of silence and withdrawal. At any rate, such difficulties augur poorly for the continuing development of a sense of trust. Not only may such dysfunctional approaches to conflict resolution become firmly entrenched over time (e.g., Kelly, Huston, & Cate, 1985), but also incidents of conflict that might under ideal circumstances set the stage for learning more about a partner's caring and responsiveness will ultimately fail in this purpose.

During the earlier evaluation stage, the primary goal of the appraisal process was to ascertain the nature of the motives and intentions behind a partner's behavior by examining its underlying symbolic significance. Although this remains the primary objective as the accommodation period begins, at this advanced stage of relationship development there is a special emphasis on satisfying a need for psychological closure regarding the partner's ultimate designs for the relationship and its future viability (Holmes, 1991). At some point a person needs to put an end to his or her uncertainty about the partner's trustworthiness and consciously act as though such confidence were rightfully deserved (Lewis & Weigert, 1985b; Rempel, Holmes, & Zanna, 1985; Silver, 1989).

Such a conviction is necessarily the result of a prospective judgment. As such, it is subject to the constraints imposed by the fact that truly conclusive evidence will forever (at least in theory) remain unattainable (Silver, 1989). The future need not necessarily mirror the past, casting serious doubt on the practicality and wisdom of basing strong expectations about things to come on evidence from the past. Rather than static and fixed in nature, relationships are fluid and variable entities that grow and change (Baxter, 1992; Brickman, 1987; Duck, 1990).

Moreover, as long as the relationship continues, there is more potentially relevant evidence that a person has not yet obtained: the array of events that are yet to come, events in which a partner may act responsively, unconscionably, unpredictably, and so on. Decades of research in social psychology attest to our only very modest ability to predict people's behavior across time and in different situations (Dawes, 1988; Ross & Nisbett, 1991).

The considerable ambivalence characteristic of the accommodation stage also renders closure a difficult psychological state to achieve (Holmes, 1991; Thompson, 1992). Ultimately, a leap of faith is required (Lewis & Weigert, 1985a, 1985b; Rempel et al., 1985). Trust becomes in some sense a construction fabricated to permit an illusion of control over areas of uncertainty that remain unresolved (cf. Janoff-Bulman, 1992; Taylor & Brown, 1988). If we are to alleviate the feelings of vulnerability that accompany such uncertainty and obstruct the pathway to comfortably trusting a partner, this construction is necessary. We must shed our indecision and forge onward, resolute in our convictions and assured in our beliefs that trust is warranted.

The Roots of Confidence: Evaluating Deservingness

In electing to trust an intimate partner, the decision is predicated on an appraisal of the evidence relating to the deservingness of the partner and the anticipated costs and benefits to be received in the relationship. Holmes and his colleagues (Boon & Holmes, 1991; Holmes, 1991; Rempel et al., 1985) articulate four key issues that partners must address in evaluating the prospects for developing within their relationship a mature capacity to trust.

Dependability

At the most elementary level, establishing a partner's dependability is fundamental to proving his or her trustworthiness. A trustworthy partner is one on whom a person can depend, who can be relied on time and time again and in all manner of situations to act honestly, considerately, and with the best of intentions. A dependable partner is reliable and consistent, the kind of person whose motives and intentions one can be certain of.

Responsiveness

Attributions of responsiveness, in contrast to attributions of dependability, extend beyond assessments of a partner's general character to his or her disposition toward the person in particular (Baier, 1986). Feelings of security in a relationship are strengthened when a partner's actions are geared toward the person's particular needs, that is, when such actions signal a special consideration of the person's needs and preferences—a unique interest in promoting a relationship with that person rather than with any other (Holmes, 1991; Reis & Shaver, 1988).

As with many other dispositions, responsiveness is best expressed in situations in which the partner's actions are counter to his or her own wishes (Holmes, 1991; Kelley, 1979; Kelley & Thibaut, 1978). By choosing to put aside his or her own preferences in order to satisfy those of the other, a partner demonstrates that he or she truly cares about the person and is intrinsically motivated in the relationship. Such self-sacrificing moves serve to validate the person's needs and desires, and to reassure him or her that the partner accepts who he or she is. According to Reis and Shaver (1988), patterns of responsiveness and validation of this sort are integral to the process by which the affectional bond between intimates is formed, maintained, and intensified.

A Capacity to Resolve Conflict

In addition to establishing that a partner is dependable and responsive, it is also necessary that a person be confident that conflicts that arise in the course of the relationship can be successfully resolved in a manner that does not either neglect partner's needs and concerns or jeopardize the relationship. If such a feeling of efficacy in the couples' ability to face conflict does not exist, the growth of trust may be seriously stunted. Issues of disagreement that remain unresolved tend to persist undiminished and resurface later in other areas, often larger and more intractable than they were initially (cf. LaFollette & Graham, 1986). Furthermore, repeated experiences of failure in a couple's efforts at problem solving are apt to generate a "terminal hypothesis" (Hurvitz, 1970), a belief that the relationship is in fact doomed to fail because the couple is unable to coordinate effective solutions to the problems they face.

Effective conflict resolution requires open and constructive engagement of the contentious issue. Such an approach affords a natural opportunity for partners to exercise their trust in each other and, through succeeding in their negotiation efforts, the opportunity to bolster their confidence in the belief that it is safe to depend on the integrity and benevolence of the other's motives (Holmes, 1991). By opening the source of their disagreement to discussion, each must assume the vulnerable stance of expressing his or her feelings to the other, boldly facing the threat of rejection or rebuff. In addition, successful problem solving typically requires some degree of compromise, some concession or self-sacrifice on the part of one or both partners. Those who dare to cross this risky terrain may emerge from the other side with a greatly intensified sense of mutual trust as their reward.

Faith

Rempel et al. (1985) describe faith as an emotionally charged sense of closure regarding the question of a partner's trustworthiness and the relationship's future. Others have described it as a construction erected to "curtail feelings of uncertainty once commitments have been made" (Boon & Holmes, 1991, p. 206), enabling an individual to extinguish any residual doubts about the partner's motives that may remain even after the criteria of dependability, responsiveness, and ability to cope with conflict have been satisfied. As discussed previously, the evidence supporting such faith can never be conclusive. Yet if a person is to feel secure relating to an intimate partner in a sometimes unsettled world, this fact must assume secondary importance to the working assumption that trust is well deserved.

Faith is linked to the extent to which an individual's view of the partner incorporates both his or her good and bad points, that is, the extent to which a person is able to come to terms with a partner's faults. When a person is able to effectively consolidate both his or her positive and negative attitudes toward the partner within a single relatively coherent and unified at- titude structure, the transformation of working hypothesis ("I hope I can trust my partner") into so-called fact ("I know I can trust my partner") eliminates the need for a vigilant appraisal process and allows feelings of insecurity and vulnerability regard- ing trust to be abandoned (Brickman, 1987; Holmes, 1991). Con- versely, when negative aspects of a partner are suppressed or denied rather than contextualized within the broader network of positive beliefs, feelings, and experiences, situations that prime such negative elements of the representation will ultimately fail to prime the wealth of positive elements that might have served to defuse the negative impact (Brickman, 1987). In this case, pockets of attributional uncertainty may remain, tagged to the isolated and compartmentalized body of negative attitudes, handi- capping a person's ability to relax his or her fears and make the leap of faith required to fully legitimize trust. Thus the success of this process of integrating the good with the bad—experien- ces of hurt and disappointment with experiences of validation and caring—may determine the breadth and depth of a person's capacity to trust (Brickman, 1987; Holmes, 1991; Janoff-Bulman, 1992).

This point is consistent with the recent views of attachment theorists (e.g., Bretherton, 1990; Main et al., 1985) who argue that "what seems to differentiate the internal working models of secure and insecure individuals is in part their content, but also *their internal organization and relative consistency within and across hierarchical levels*" (Bretherton, 1990, p. 247, italics added). In contrast to insecure individuals, those who feel com- fortable and secure relating closely to others and depending on them are characterized by an apparent integration of both the positive and negative aspects of their experiences.

Calm Seas and Crises of Confidence:
The Fabric of Trust in Established Relationships

Few relationships survive the road to an established and maintained mutual trust without encountering dilemmas that pose a potential threat to their security. The above discussion of the bases of trust highlights the assortment of issues on which people's sense of security in a relationship may be challenged (Boon & Holmes, 1991). Whereas some couples are able to surmount the tribulations they face and emerge from each struggle with an intensified confidence in their ability to depend on each other, others are unable to quell their anxieties sufficiently to permit such confidence to firmly take root.

Attitudes and expectations about a partner's motives born of such experiences are likely to color the interpretation of later relationship events (e.g., Reis & Shaver, 1988). Consistent with this assumption, a sizable literature substantiates the premise that the act of social perception—on which our expectations and attitudes are based—is itself essentially a constructive process (Kelvin, 1977; La Gaipa, 1987; Miller & Turnbull, 1986). The notion that we are not the objective, accurate, information processors we often think ourselves to be is a well-documented empirical fact (see also Gilbert, 1989; Kruglanski, 1990; Kunda, 1990; Ross & Nisbett, 1991). Often a range of biases and perceptual distortions acting in the service of our perceptual agendas ensure that what we see is what we expect.

Furthermore, adopting a more rhetorical stance, it is clear that we possess considerable ability to choose the labels and meanings we apply to a partner's actions (e.g., Billig, 1987). According to this point of view there are always (at least) two perspectives from which we may view any event or incident, neither of which is unequivocally and irrevocably correct. An act that some may consider inexcusably arrogant and selfish others may view as legitimately self-confident and rightly self-interested. In other words, the data with which partners are faced in their relationships does not restrict them to a single interpretation—nor does it preclude appreciable flexibility in inference. As Dixson and Duck (1993) state, "Natural phenomena do not scream out at us to be interpreted in a particular way; they make rather subliminal whispers" (p. 180).

In consequence, an act may be construed in a multiplicity of ways and, furthermore, such construals may change and shift over time as the context of thought within which they are embedded also changes (Duck, 1990). This is true, Kelvin (1977) claims, because attributions such as whether a partner is trustworthy or not have their causal locus in the perceiver, not the perceived. That is, trustworthiness, in this important sense, is an attributed property rather than a revealed property (see also Duck, 1990; La Gaipa, 1987). In this final section I consider the nature of the appraisal process as it functions in established relationships, characterizing the fabric of experience for those able to overcome successfully the challenges of depending on another as well as for those less able to brave the sometimes stormy seas of intimacy.

Trusting Relationships

A sense of confidence pervades the relationships of those who have successfully achieved a comparatively full capacity to trust each other, liberating them from ever-mounting pressures to evade feelings of vulnerability and doubt (Holmes, 1991). Their faith in each other well established, theirs is an intimacy free from the shadows of doubt and uncertainty that otherwise might threaten their sense of assurance in the relationship (Boon & Holmes, 1991; Holmes, 1991).

A charitable orientation toward evaluating the partner's actions is perhaps the essential hallmark of a trusting relationship. In part this liberal view of the partner's behaviors and underlying motives is due to the long-term nature of the accounting process that trusting individuals employ to track their partners' contributions to the relationship. Evaluated within the broader context of positive events and experiences the couple has shared over a fairly protracted period of time, occasional negative behaviors inevitably pale in significance. Such an extended perspective indeed tends to have a stabilizing effect on people's perceptions of the course of the relationship (Holmes, 1991), smoothing the peaks and valleys in the contours of the relationship experience; the impact of a single selfish or inconsiderate act is attenuated by the aggregation of an extensive array of events within which it is embedded. Unfortunately, the impact of any single act of caring is similarly moderated by virtue of being interpreted in the broader scheme of things. This has the somewhat unanticipated consequence of ensuring that positive acts or events often are taken for granted (see also Berscheid, 1983).

The poetic license with which trusting persons interpret a partner's behavior is also a function of the manner in which they approach the inference process (Holmes, 1991) when situations demand an actual appraisal. Because the person is armed with a set of confident expectations about the inherently intrinsic and caring nature of his or her partner's motives, hypothesis testing proceeds in a manner that virtually guarantees at the outset that the outcome will conform to initial expectations.

First, with optimistic expectations guiding the inferential processing in a top-down fashion, a bias toward distorting the evidence in a favorable direction is likely to culminate in a conclusion that justifies the faith placed in the partner. Any signs indicative of positive motives are likely to be accepted unequivocally, and the implications and significance of negative acts can be defused in a number of ways without disturbing the fabric of the conviction that trust is deserved. For example, an inconsiderate act might be explained away in dispositional or situational terms that bear few implications for attributions about the relationship itself (e.g., "He doesn't talk much because he's the strong silent type. But that's what makes him such a supportive partner."). Alternatively, the implications of such an act might be relegated to some peripheral area of concern where they have little impact on issues of larger significance. Such modes of explanation function to preserve feelings of security, in a sense serving to discount negative acts before they occur (Boon & Holmes, 1991).

In addition, by framing the question in abstract, conclusional terms ("Can I trust my partner?") but proceeding to answer it with evidence obtained at a lower, more concrete act or behavior level ("Is this act inconsiderate?"), considerable latitude may be exercised in establishing the range and type of behaviors deemed acceptable proof of trustworthy, caring motives (Holmes, 1991). Consistent with this argument, preliminary evidence (Boon, 1992) suggests that people may be inclined toward more generous inferences about a partner at the more abstract conclusion level (i.e., pertaining to the significance and implications of the act for the relationship generally) than at the level of interpreting the behavior as an act in a particular instance. Specifically, people were more disapproving in their act-level interpretations of a particular behavior in the context in which it occurred than in the broader, more general conclusions they were willing to draw on the basis of that behavior. Intriguingly, this pattern of divergent attributions at the two levels of inference was exacerbated when the experimental conditions made salient the risks associated with becoming involved in a romantic relationship.

Empirical support also substantiates the compelling notion that, in circumstances in which trusting individuals are indeed forced to confront evidence discrepant with their trusting orientation, they actually may come to view their partner's behavior and motives in an even more positive light than had they stopped to consider expectation-consistent behavior (Holmes & Rempel, 1989). In activating the negative elements of the representational structure of the relationship, the act of considering the significance of the negative behavior may simultaneously prime the associated positive elements and consequently provide trusting individuals with precisely the evidence needed to resolve the dilemma posed by the discrepant act (Brickman, 1987; Holmes, 1991). When they defeat the challenge in this manner, their sense of personal satisfaction may be amplified correspondingly.

Finally, additional research suggests the hypothesis that high-trust individuals' memories regarding the motives and intentions underlying a partner's negative behaviors may become more positive in tone as time passes (Holmberg & Holmes, in press). Indeed, trust was strongly and positively related to the degree of charitable bias in the recall of both positive and negative events, even after attributions provided at the time of the event were taken into consideration. Furthermore, one month later those events originally rated most severe and negative were rated least likely to have wide-ranging repercussions throughout the relationship.

Altogether, trusting relationships are characterized by an absence of open concern about issues of trust and security. Trust is to some extent implicit in such relationships, a natural extension of each partner's love and concern for the other and their assurance that their feelings are mutual. Whether in practice such unswerving faith is ever truly justified, it grants trusting individuals the capacity to face the uncertain prospects for the future of their relationship with optimism, hope, and equanimity.

When Trust Fails

For a variety of reasons, however, not all relationships can attain this ideal standard. Acts perceived as less than wholly benevolent or unselfish that some might be able to reconstrue rather harmlessly as instances of charming irregularity or unreliablity may prove for others considerable obstacles to maintaining trust. Sometimes the stack of evidence apparently disproving a partner's trustworthiness accumulates until it reaches a point at which it may seem almost incontrovertible. After repeated experiences of disappointment or even betrayal in episodes involving trust, a person might decide that the risk and emotional toll associated with continued trusting are simply too great to justify the effort. The threshold of tolerance having been exceeded by an accumulated debt of violated expectations (Holmes, 1991), a crisis of confidence may occur and alternative mechanisms may be implemented to deal with situations that prime feelings of vulnerability. Such mechanisms ultimately serve the purpose of decreasing the degree of interdependence in the relationship, in a move to protect against future risk and pain.

A sort of defensive pessimism is primary among the self-protective mechanisms employed by people whose trust has eroded (Holmes, 1991). By expecting the worst, they are psychologically prepared for any eventuality and can stave off anxieties stemming from a fear of venturing to trust again. Unfortunately, this rather close-minded approach—first concluding that a partner is untrustworthy and then letting this assumption guide the appraisal process—often serves only to confirm their negative expectations, bolstering a belief that trust is undeserved (Baier, 1986; Thomas, 1978). The result is a tendency toward distorting a partner's behavior in a negative direction, a process rather the mirror image of that employed by trusting individuals (Holmes, 1991). Because such a person is vigilant for signs of selfishness and lack of caring, whatever residual seeds of hope he or she still may cling to are likely to be quashed by fears about the consequences of drawing yet another unwarranted positive conclusion about the partner's motives (Holmes, 1991; Kruglanski, 1990). Accordingly, positive acts are viewed with considerable skepticism, effectively diminishing their perceived significance and utility (e.g., Holtzworth-Munroe & Jacobson, 1985), and acts of a more ambiguous nature are recast in uncomplimentary, disparaging terms.

The impact of a partner's negative acts also is enhanced by a restricted focus on the rather immediate balance of exchange within the relationship. When a partner's motives are considered suspect, this distrustful orientation to the accounting process is likely to be activated by concerns about being taken advantage of. Because evidence of reciprocity is tracked within a very narrow time frame, even fairly small imbalances may attract considerable attention, adding to the perceived need to exercise caution in the relationship.

All in all, the erosion of trust typically sets in motion a vicious cycle in which doubts and pessimistic expectations fuel a defensive, self-protective style of processing that tends to be self-perpetuating. Although in theory this process is not irreversible,

in practice once initiated its own momentum is likely to produce
an escalation rather than a reduction in the rate at which any
remaining shreds of trust deteriorate.

Under what conditions and at what point does an act (or a series
of acts) come to be viewed as a betrayal? When is enough enough?
Little is known about the processes guiding this crucial transition point in the appraisal of a partner's actions. Research does
indicate, however, that even many decades later such interpersonal events may retain much of their symbolic impact (Hansson,
Jones, & Fletcher, 1990). Furthermore, it is wise to note that "the
immense potential for seemingly innocent or unthinking actions to be experienced as betrayal [suggests] how easily it could
happen in almost any family or relationship" (Hansson et al., 1990,
p. 457).

Living in the Shadow of Doubt

Some people find themselves caught between the two extremes
depicted above, unable to sustain an unfaltering conviction that
the partner is trustworthy, yet at the same time optimistic that
such a supposition is true. Lingering anxieties and feelings of
vulnerability weave a web of uncertainty and ambivalence from
which such people often find it exceedingly difficult to untangle
themselves. When situations conspire to challenge the reserves
of confidence they have built up over time, they are led to re-
instate an active appraisal process in an effort to lay their fears
to rest once and for all. Unfortunately, such efforts rarely are
effective in securing their objective (Holmes, 1991).

Considerable emotional involvement leads uncertain individuals to be hopeful that they can find grounds on which to base
confident expectations that their partner is truly caring, yet
pockets of vulnerability simultaneously pull them away from any
decisive conclusion in this direction. The potential costs associated with incorrectly concluding that a partner is benevolently
motivated leave them simply unwilling to take that risk (Holmes,
1991; Kruglanski, 1990). Accordingly, they find themselves en-
snared within a seemingly intractable approach-avoidance con-

flict: Despite an apparent longing to banish their uncertainty regarding the partner's motives, they are reluctant to pronounce any verdict on the issue, preferring instead to wait until an over-abundance of favorable evidence compels them to do so (Boon & Holmes, 1991; Kruglanski, 1990).

There are at least two fundamental problems with this ap-praisal process as it operates in relationships in which trust remains an open concern, both of which may be seen to stem from the above tendency toward risk aversion (Holmes, 1991). First, apprehensions about the prohibitive price of drawing an unjustified charitable inference are likely to lead uncertain in-dividuals to frame the test of trustworthiness in a negative manner, expecting at any moment to find their fears empirically substantiated. With such pessimistic expectations at the helm of the hypothesis-testing process, the outcome is liable to cor-roborate their initial assumption that a decision to trust is a choice to expose themselves to unwanted risk.

Such risk-aversive tendencies also result in an asymmetry in the balance of evidence required to substantiate a positive versus a negative conclusion, the criteria employed to evaluate the evidence obtained in the appraisal process. Due to their reluc-tance to err in the direction of drawing a favorable but incorrect conclusion, uncertain individuals adopt rigorous criteria for accepting positive behaviors as truly diagnostic of caring and unselfish motives (Boon, 1992). In the same way that a scientist might employ a conservative alpha level to minimize the likeli-hood of a Type I error, these individuals adopt stringent criteria in judging the perceived merit of behaviors that are consistent with their hopes (Holmes, 1991). Equivocal evidence is deemed inadequate to the purpose. Comparatively lenient, the criteria imposed on negative behaviors serve to complement an uncer-tain individual's negative expectations.

Because of this rather skeptical orientation, the larger mean-ing and significance of positive behaviors are viewed with sus-picion and doubt, whereas the broader implications of negative acts are rather readily entertained. The outcome is a tendency toward conservative inferences, and toward conclusions that shy away from being unequivocally charitable. Consistent with this line of reasoning, Holmes and Rempel (1989) found that uncertain people were hesitant to grant a partner credit for his or her benevolent acts, yet quite prepared to blame the partner's motives for any negative behaviors committed. Additional evidence suggests that the perceived price to be paid if a benevolent attribution is drawn may, paradoxically, increase as a person approaches the point of actually obtaining evidence indicating such an attribution is warranted. Uncertain individuals were significantly more negative in their evaluations of a partner's motives after recalling a positive event in their relationship than after recalling a negative event (Holmes & Rempel, 1989).

Uncertain individuals also often find themselves drawn into a relatively short-term accounting process (Holmes, 1991) in conditions in which the appraisal process is reactivated. Among trusting persons an exchange ledger based on a relatively long-term perspective affords an appearance of balance, attenuating the impact of any single event; the rather more narrow time frame that uncertain persons employ robs them of this opportunity for the passage of time and the aggregation of events to level out the peaks and valleys of their experience. Consequently, whereas trusting individuals may be recognized by the stability and calm evident in their reactions to everyday events, individuals whose beliefs about their partner's motives are plagued by unresolved uncertainty tend instead to be relatively more volatile and reactive.

Interpreted within a fairly localized context that may bear little resemblance to the fabric of the broader network of relationship experiences, reactions to both positive and negative events are considerably amplified by this restricted perspective (Holmes, 1991). Because they focus on the moment-by-moment transactions within their relationship, it becomes more difficult for uncertain individuals to dismiss the implications of acts that are uncaring, selfish, or inconsiderate. They also are less able to restrict the damage of any single thoughtless or hurtful act to areas of peripheral importance. Evaluated in relative isolation, such events will tend to acquire a symbolic meaning all their own, often far exceeding the significance they would have attained had they been considered within a wider context (Holmes, 1991). Positive acts similarly will command greater attention than they might have if a longer-term perspective were employed; however, tendencies that were noted above will serve to keep their impact in check.

Thus where vestiges of vulnerability and uncertainty remain there exists a complex dilemma. Caught amidst conflicting hopes and fears, uncertain individuals struggle to unearth conclusive evidence regarding a partner's motives. Unhappily, to the degree that their fears about rejection have rendered them unable to achieve an effective and coherent consolidation of their positive and negative attitudes toward the partner, they are vulnerable to the sorts of biased information-processing tendencies described above, tendencies that ultimately constrain the effectiveness of their attempts to reduce their feelings of uncertainty.

Conclusion

I began this chapter by discussing the risk and vulnerability that attend the development and maintenance of trust within relationships, attempting to locate such processes within the broader context of relationship phenomena both "light" and "dark." I conclude by recapitulating my argument that such a perspective captures much of the experience of trusting a romantic partner, the dialectic tension between partners' hopes and fears. As I have sought to illustrate, the seeds of mutual trust often grow best in risky soil, where the prospects for the relationship are to some extent uncertain and unpleasant consequences might await those who proceed onward. The means by which partners negotiate the dilemmas they face as their relationship progresses shape the nature of the bond of trust between them. At the same time, this trust also shapes their perceptions of the situations they encounter and the strategies they invoke to deal with these situations. Trust and risk are thus intimately related: The continually changing juxtaposition of these two elements in any relationship may portend well or ill for its future course.

5

Similarities and Dissimilarities in Personal Relationships: Constructing Meaning and Building Intimacy Through Communication

Michael Monsour

A s this volume and series make clear, any relational behavior can be understood from different perspectives and is part of a complex process as well as a topic in its own right. Against that background this chapter focuses on the cognitive and interactional competencies involved (a) in communicating knowledge about oneself during the course of an interaction and (b) in managing and acquiring knowledge about one's relational partner, and on the mutual communicative integration of that knowledge into a coherent and at least partially shared relational whole. Specifically, I review the effects of communicating about similarity and dissimilarity on the evolution of understanding and intimacy in a relationship. In reviewing those effects the similarity construct is closely scrutinized and expanded. Theoretical amplification of the similarity construct reveals that the competent communication and comprehension of dis/similarities result in the sharing of meaning between relational partners. When individuals share meaning they have taken the first step toward establishing a "symbolic union," a union that will promote understanding and the perception of order in a relational universe that frequently is characterized by chaos and a lack of predictability (Duck & Barnes, 1992). Mutual understanding of similarities and differences between relational partners facilitates a shared perceptual reality, a reality that may encourage or deter the pursuit of intimacy in the relationship.

Effects of Communicating
About Similarity and Dissimilarity

There are numerous possible effects of communicating about dis/similarity, particularly when similarity is viewed as a "social process" rather than as a "cognitive state of affairs" (Duck, 1994a). Before reviewing those effects it is necessary to stipulate what types of similarity merit our attention in this chapter. Relational partners can be similar in a multitude of ways, but not all of those similarities are communicated, nor do they all have an appreciable impact on intimacy development. I am specifically concerned with those types of dis/similarities that influence the development of intimacy in a relationship, and that can be discovered and revealed by relational partners through communication. Once dis/similarities are discovered or revealed, whether intentionally or fortuitously, talk about those dis/similarities influences the way they are incorporated into individual and dyadic definitions of the relationship (Acitelli, 1993). In line with the emphases of this series and this volume, therefore, I focus on the communicative consequences and the dynamic processes that surround dis/similarity.

Communicating About Attitude Similarity:
Byrne Revisited

As a starting point in reviewing the effects of communicating about dis/similarity I focus on verbal communication about attitude similarity. The most obvious and investigated effect of communicating about attitude similarity is that it might lead to increased attraction between partners. The notion that attitude similarity augments interpersonal attraction is an ancient one, beginning with Aristotle's essay on friendship (330 B.C.E./1932). In a historical sketch of the attitude similarity-attraction relationship, Byrne (1992) gives credit to dozens of studies that preceded his own thinking on the subject of similarity and attraction (e.g., Newcomb, 1956; Smith, 1957). However, Byrne's work served as the catalyst for substantial research and controversy on the relationship between attitude similarity and attraction, and how communication between partners influences that relationship (Byrne, 1961, 1971). Though the vast majority of Byrne's research does not explicitly focus on communication, he may have unwittingly contributed to the view that communication is unproblematic in the effects of dis/similarity (S. W. Duck, personal communication, August 15, 1993).

In a nutshell, Byrne, a reinforcement theorist, was interested in determining the effect of attitude dis/similarity on attraction between strangers. Byrne recognized from the beginning that many other variables were associated with attraction, and that attitude similarity would not always be the most important of those variables (Byrne, 1961, 1992). To isolate the effects of attitude similarity on attraction Byrne developed his now famous (or to some, infamous) "bogus stranger" research design. In the most commonly known and criticized variation of the bogus-stranger method, a subject fills out an attitude survey and is later shown another survey that presumably was completed by a stranger. The subject then would respond to a two-item Interpersonal Judgment Scale (Byrne, 1961) indicating how attracted he or she was to the stranger. The higher the level of agreement between the subject's scale and that of the bogus stranger, the higher the level of attraction the subject would report toward that stranger. In actuality, however, there was no stranger (hence the bogus stranger). The experimenter had completed the stranger's scale so it would correspond with the subject's to some given degree so that the effects of degree of similarity could be precisely assessed. Specifically, attraction toward a stranger varied as a linear function of the "proportion of weighted units of positive affect (the sum of the weighted units of positive affect divided by the sum of the weighted units of positive and negative affect)" (Byrne, 1992, p. 192).

Over the years Byrne and his colleagues employed numerous permutations of this basic design, but in all of them attraction toward a stranger was found to be a linear function of the proportion of similar and dissimilar attitudes between an individual and that stranger (Byrne, Ervin, & Lamberth, 1970; Byrne & Griffitt, 1966). Byrne contends that though attitude similarity is usually rewarding, and dissimilarity is usually punishing, it is not because of some unique quality inherent in dis/similarity. Rather it is the meaning assigned by an individual to the stimulus that makes it attractive or aversive (Byrne & Lamberth, 1971, p. 66). If the meaning and/or significance of the similarity is altered by some other variable in the social context then similarity may not lead to attraction (Byrne, 1971; Byrne & Lamberth, 1971; Duck & Barnes, 1992).

Since the initial bogus-stranger research a large and growing body of literature supports the hypothesis that attitude similarity leads to increased interpersonal attraction. Indeed, Cappella and Palmer (1990) conclude that "perhaps the most well known and well established finding in the study of interpersonal relations is that attitude similarity creates attraction" (p. 161). As Bochner (1991) incredulously observed, other researchers echo the same sentiments as Cappella and Palmer (e.g., Berscheid & Walster, 1978). However not all scholars studying this phenomenon agree that attitude similarity leads to attraction. Many have offered alternative explanations for the attitude similarity-attraction effect (e.g., Aronson & Worchel, 1966; Rodin, 1982; Rosenbaum, 1986). Some authors have been quite caustic in their commentaries, labeling the attitude similarity-attraction effect a "myth" (Sunnafrank, 1991, 1992) and calling for the "death" of the attitude similarity-attraction paradigm (Bochner, 1991).

For purposes of this chapter, relevant criticisms and extensions of the attraction paradigm are those that attempt to explain the part played by communication in the similarity-attraction process. The most well known and controversial investigations are those conducted by Michael Sunnafrank. In a series of studies Sunnafrank (Sunnafrank, 1983, 1984; Sunnafrank & Miller, 1981) attempted to demonstrate that interaction washes out the effects of attitude similarity on attraction. In three studies, previously unacquainted conversational partners were paired on the basis of dis/similarity on two controversial topics. Partners were under the impression that they would be working with one another on a project involving those topics. Each participant was made aware of the attitudes of his or her partner on those two topics. Individuals in the no-interaction condition were then given a variation of Byrne's Interpersonal Judgment Scale. Those in the interaction condition first engaged in a 5-minute get-acquainted conversation with their partner. The 5-minute conversation attenuated the effects of attitude similarity, whereas those who had not interacted continued to demonstrate the attitude similarity-attraction relationship. The attenuation effect occurred in studies in which participants were instructed not to discuss the topics during the 5-minute conversation (Sunnafrank, 1983), as well as when they were asked to discuss the controversial topic (Sunnafrank, 1984). In all of these studies interaction led to increased attraction toward individuals with dissimilar attitudes, but not toward those with similar ones.

Sunnafrank's work has been subjected to trenchant criticism for employing a weak manipulation of attitude dis/similarity, for not actually coding any of the interaction, and for having the interlocutors interact for only 5 minutes (Cappella & Palmer, 1990, 1992). Despite their criticisms, Cappella and Palmer agree with Sunnafrank that interaction has a dampening effect on the attitude similarity-attraction relationship—though, they argue, the effect is a limited one. Their major concern, as is mine in this chapter, was to determine how, when, and why the mitigating effects of communication occur.

In an effort to improve, expand, and further test ideas put forward by Sunnafrank, Cappella and Palmer (1990) had conversational partners converse for 30 minutes in which vocal and kinesic behaviors were coded to determine whether those behaviors could account for some of the mediating effects of communication on attraction. They hypothesized that individuals who experience similarity during an interaction would display more involving nonverbal behaviors than would those who are dissimilar. Indeed, certain nonverbal behaviors indicating involvement had a direct, though complicated, impact on level of attraction. In some cases nonverbal behaviors and similarity both served to increase attraction, and results indicated that similarity in nonverbal behaviors not only explained variance in attraction ratings, but also wiped out the effects of attitude similarity on attraction. Cappella and Palmer see this last finding as particularly important because it affirms Sunnafrank's hypothesis that communication negates the effects of attitude similarity on attraction, while at the same time it explains the actual interactional mechanisms that lead to the attenuating effects of communication on the attitude similarity-attraction relationship.

One oversight of the Cappella and Palmer (1990) study deserves mentioning because it is indicative of shortcomings in other studies examining the effects of similarity on attraction. Half of the subjects were instructed to select a partner who had similar opinions, beliefs, attitudes, and values. Though some scholars (Campbell, 1963) argue that values and attitudes are synonymous because the attitude object has valence, others contend that values are not tied to any specific attitude object or situation (Rokeach, 1972). The point is not so much that scholars display a lack of similarity as to the difference between values and attitudes, but rather that laypersons participating in research might differentiate between those constructs. Communication of similar attitudes could play a minor role in attraction if value dissimilarity exists and overshadows the effects of attitude similarity.

The topic of value similarity points to the usefulness of a brief discussion of the role played by personality similarity on attraction. Duck (1976) argues that one of the primary purposes of the acquaintance process is to acquire information about the partner's personality in order to assess the degree of similarity to oneself as a means to verify and support one's own hypotheses about the world. When an individual discovers personality similarities, those similarities serve to validate one's own personality structure. There are various levels at which a relational partner's personality might be assessed, and similarities at different levels, such as an individual's personal value system, are more salient during different stages of relational development (Duck & Craig, 1978).

Burleson and Denton (1992) offer another alternative explanation of the attitude similarity-attraction relationship. They argue that once individuals become engaged in interaction they are not as concerned with attitude similarity as they are with just trying to enjoy the interaction, and that it is similarity in social skills that enhances attraction. Studying marital couples, Burleson and Denton (1992) found support for their contention that communication-based variables, such as similarity in communication style, can account for interpersonal attraction better than attitude similarity can.

Another criticism of Byrne's paradigm and the attitude similarity-attraction relationship focuses on the temporal sequence of that relationship. Bochner (1991) maintains that it is more logical to think that attraction precedes similarity rather than follows it. According to Bochner's reasoning, individuals assume that they and their relational partners should have things in common, and therefore communicate in ways to foster the impression of similarity. This sounds very much like a self-fulfilling prophecy (Merton, 1948), in which an individual has certain expectations about how a partner should be, and then proceeds to act in ways that will cause the partner to confirm those expectations. Thus initial attraction to an individual for reasons other than attitude similarity, such as loneliness, might

lead to behavior that encourages the revealing and/or construction of similarities in hopes of facilitating a friendship.

Another limitation of Byrne's attraction paradigm, as well as
many of the studies it inspired (e.g., Cappella & Palmer, 1990;
Sunnafrank & Miller, 1981), is illustrated by those situations in
which attitudes and values are not straightforwardly communicated, and in which persons are not privy to the attitudes of their
partner before the interaction. In much of the research on the
attitude similarity-attraction relationship, knowledge of attitude
dis/similarity existed prior to interaction (usually supplied by a
well-meaning researcher), rather than being revealed, discovered,
cajoled, and constructed by relational participants as the interaction unfolded. Conversational partners in the early stages of a
relationship have a general tendency to avoid controversial topics
and potential areas of disagreement, which in turn may give the
impression of more similarity than actually exists (Sunnafrank,
1986). Even in well-established relationships with a rich history
of attitudinal exchanges, partners might be motivated to reveal
some dis/similarities and conceal others (Sunnafrank, 1991). Of
considerable interest to relationship scholars are those situations in which individuals do not wish to communicate certain
information.

Along these lines, when cognizant of dissimilarties, relational
partners may downplay those differences by using communication strategies such as equivocation (Bavelas, Black, Chovil, &
Mullett, 1990) and politeness (Brown & Levinson, 1987). The
capacity to glean attitudes and values from conversations cloaked
in equivocation and politeness is a competency worthy of close
scrutiny, as is the companion ability of skillfully masking attitudes and values under a veneer of vague and courteous conversation. As recently defined (Bavelas et al., 1990), equivocation
occurs when part of a message disqualifies another part, leading
to the possibility of multiple interpretations of that message.
Individuals equivocate when they perceive that "all other communicative choices would lead to negative consequences" (Bavelas
et al., 1990, p. 54). To free oneself from this dilemma the individual equivocates. Equivocation does not necessarily mean a

true opinion is not being stated. In their critique of the deception literature, Bavelas and her associates (1990) observe that deception research seems to be based on the assumption that individuals frequently lie. To the contrary, Bavelas and her colleagues argue that when given a choice individuals would rather truthfully equivocate than deceive. This propensity for equivocation makes the detection of salient dis/similarities a difficult task. From a competency perspective, a competent communicator might be one who can skillfully equivocate when the situation demands it, and also have the ability to glean underlying attitudes and values from an individual who is equivocating. Among other things, skillful equivocation is when an individual is able to equivocate in such a way that the partner trusts that the equivocation is an attempt to strengthen the relationship, rather than to undermine it. Interpersonal trust exists when an individual is confident that his or her partner is intrinsically motivated to act in that individual's own best interest (Boon, Chapter 4 in this volume).

Politeness is another communicative strategy that makes the detection of dis/similarities a sometimes formidable endeavor. An individual engaging in a "positive politeness" strategy during interaction might look for safe topics in order to seek agreement with a partner and establish common ground (Brown & Levinson, 1987). Though on the surface this appears to be a relatively innocuous tactic to employ in interaction, such a strategy might encourage the perception of more similarity than actually exists and foster a false sense of similarity. On a related matter, if an individual suspects that an expressed similarity may merely reflect politeness, he or she may generate numerous causal attributions as to why such information was communicated. This would be more likely if the similarity was an "unexpected outcome" (Fletcher & Fitness, 1993).

The use of politeness as a strategy has a direct link to "dialectical complexities" in the area of competency. Spitzberg (1993) delineates a number of dialectical tensions operating in the attempted employment of competent communication. The most relevant for our concerns involves the choice between short- and long-term goals. Seeking out safe topics in conversation with a relational partner may help reach the short-term goal of easy interaction, but it also might interfere with a long-term goal of establishing a relationship based on an accurate understanding of both similarities and dissimilarities.

To protect themselves against interactional strategies such as equivocation and politeness, relational partners might employ the cognitive strategy of second-guessing. In this strategy the hearer of a message consciously employs one or more interpretive frameworks in an attempt to remove bias from a message, with the hope of extracting more accurate information from the message than it contains if taken at face value (Hewes & Planalp, 1982). For example, if an individual's relational partner begins to equivocate during discussion of some salient issue, that individual might reinterpret the message (i.e., second-guess), and then proceed to employ any number of communicative strategies (Berger, 1993) to test that reinterpretation.

In addition to similarities in nonverbal styles, thus far the discussion of the effects of communicating about similarity has focused on attitude and value similarities. However, similarities between relational partners also might be manifested in the more transient state, as opposed to trait, conditions of the relational partners (Ickes, Tooke, Stinson, Baker, & Bissonnette, 1988). Attitudes and values are considered to be relatively stable dispositions, or traits. On the other hand, thoughts and feelings at any given time are less stable and reflect the particular state an individual is in during the interaction. The ability to accurately communicate the thoughts and feelings one is experiencing during an interaction, which is part of empathic communication (Ickes et al., 1988), and the ability to correctly infer the content of another person's thoughts and feelings (empathic accuracy) are fundamental to competency. If partners are experiencing similar thoughts and feelings during an interaction the communication of those commonalities would be central to establishing connectiveness between the partners.

**Theoretical Amplification
of the Similarity Construct**

A substantial part of the difficulty in ascertaining the effects of communicating about dis/similarity on relational development is that commentators have failed to adequately delineate the similarity construct, and how it fits into the larger "social transactive context" (Duck, 1994a). In an evolving explication of the similarity construct, Duck (1994a) presents a model of the "serial construction of meaning," in which similarity refers not only to similarity in attitudes and values, but to a similarity in the organizational structure of meaning as well (see Figure 5.1). In Duck's model similarity is a process rather than a state, with various levels at which it can exist and have impact on relational partners. In a serial progression the model includes commonality, mutuality, equivalence, and sharing.

Commonalities exist between individuals when both independently have done the same sorts of things, and/or have the same attitude toward some X. For example, P and O may belong to the same environmental group and have similar attitudes toward that group. At the point of mere commonality, relational partners are not aware of the existence of these commonalities and dissimilarities, illustrating the pivotal distinction between being similar and the realization of similarity—a distinction that has not been fully acknowledged by Byrne and other commentators (Duck & Barnes, 1992). Though realization of commonality is sometimes an individual cognitive endeavor (Laing, Phillipson, & Lee, 1966), that realization becomes more meaningful if it is engendered and shared through talk. Once individuals talk about their commonalities through "declaration" (i.e., self-disclosure) or observe them in one another, a mutual past is created (Katovich & Couch, 1992). Part of mutuality is the joint recognition that the partners share certain commonalities. Crucial to the model is the "evaluation" of those commonalities, in which partners appraise how each interprets the things they have in common. During evaluation one or both partners assess the degree to which they each construe the commonality in an equivalent fashion. If

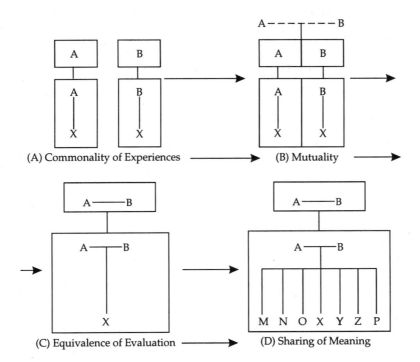

Figure 5.1. A Model of the Serial Construction of Meaning

SOURCE: See also Duck, S. W. (1994a). *Meaningful relationships: Talking, sense, and re-lating* (Sage Series on Close Relationships, Vol. 8). Thousand Oaks, CA: Sage.
NOTE: Figure 5.1 represents the progressively developing constructions of two partners about each other in relation to topic X. In commonality the two persons, A and B, relate to topic X but do so independently of one another. In mutuality they now know that the same topic is in the experience of each of them (experience = events). In equivalence they both see, further, how they evaluate X (experience = subjective interpretation). In sharing they see how they evaluate not only X but also several other topics, events, and experiences that contextualize their evaluation of X (i.e., they have a common organization for meaning surrounding topic X). The figure does not depict one process, but depicts the general process that continues with different foci during all the unfinished business of relating.

they interpret the commonality in the same way, then they have an underlying "equivalence of values." For example, if two individuals each were independently arrested for protesting at a nuclear test site they have a "common past" (Katovich & Couch,

1992). Though their commonality is an important similarity, of greater importance is how each interprets or construes the common event. For one individual, being arrested may have been a negative experience for self-image, whereas for the other it might have been a positive one. If they both evaluate it in the same way, they are equivalent in their interpretation of the experience. Sharing occurs when the individuals realize that they equivalently view not only X (in this case, being arrested at the protest), but also other Xs that contextualize their evaluation of X. To use Duck's (1994a) words, "They have a common organization for meaning surrounding topic X." So in this example, the partners may have dis/similarity concerning their views on the reasons for the protest, the arresting officers, press coverage of the event, familial reaction to their arrests, and so on.

In Duck's delineation a distinction is drawn between elements that are external and internal to the relationship. Though elements external to a relationship (such as the nuclear protest example) certainly have some bearing on relational dynamics, they are not as significant as are those that have direct application to the relationship. For example, P and O may have common pasts in that they both have been taken advantage of in past friendships. In the process of becoming friends they each may relate their unpleasant past experiences. During this declaration phase they realize that they share certain beliefs and attitudes about how friends should treat one another. As they share those beliefs and attitudes they are implicitly defining the parameters of their evolving friendship.

Duck further argues that the discovery and sharing of a specific commonality, and thus the recognition of a similarity, might lead individuals to further discourse and the assumption (hope?) that the commonality might be extended to other areas. Though individuals may be similar in specific areas, the underlying importance of those similarities is how they are indicative of broader areas of psychological similarity that might exist between individuals. Discussion of dis/similarities might lead to subsequent discovery of other types of similarity at various levels of psychological organization. The mutual perception of layers of similarity is continually modified in an attempt to establish a joint perceptual view of the relationship.

To the extent that individuals have similar perceptual views of their relationship, they also might have similar relational schemas (Andersen, 1993; Planalp, 1985). As defined by Planalp (1985), relational schemata are "coherent frameworks of relational knowledge which are used to derive relational implications of messages and are modified in accord with ongoing experiences with relationships" (p. 9). The relational schema guides communication with the partner, and communication in turn affects the content and structuring of the schema (Planalp, 1985).

The relational schema construct has clear implications for the effects of communicating about dis/similarity. An individual's schema for a particular type of relationship, such as friendship, might suggest that friends should have similarities, but that they also should accept and appreciate differences. In a specific friendship schema (meaning one with a specific person) various types of dis/similarities are stored. These dis/similarities might actually exist, or they may be inaccurate perceptions based on inferences generated from one's schema. Communication with a relational partner might validate or invalidate those perceived commonalities and incongruencies, leading to a restructuring of one's schema. The key is that the individuals must talk about those areas. Similarity of specific relational schemata between two individuals, as long as they recognize it, is pivotal in the construction of a mutually understood relational reality.

Transactive memory is instrumental in the formation of similar relational schemata between partners. As recently delineated, transactive memory involves a variety of processes that allow information to enter a relationship to be organized within that relationship, and to be subsequently utilized by one or both relational partners (Wegner et al., 1985). Transactive memory entails the individual and joint knowledge structures that each partner has concerning their relationship and "can be said to reside in the memories of both individuals—when they are considered as a combined system" (Wegner et al., 1985, p. 257).

Interactive processes that occur between relational partners, typically manifested as communication, are an essential element of transactive memory. For example, when partners are reminiscing about some past event in their relationship, each might remember different parts of that event. Through a process known as "interactive cuing" (Wegner et al., 1985) their individual memories may serve as cues to stimulate more remembrances from one another concerning the event. Between the two individuals they are able to reasonably reconstruct the event, or at least their perception of the event.

Though several of the processes involved in transactive memory have direct relevance to our discussion of the effects of communicating about similarity, one is of particular importance. The previously discussed extension construct (Duck, 1994a) has implications for an encoding phenomenon known as semantic elaboration (Anderson & Reder, 1979). Semantic elaboration occurs when inferences are drawn about incoming information, and when that information is related to knowledge already stored. For example, when a similarity is communicated to a relational partner, that partner might elaborate on the information by extending it to other types of similarity, or to other layers of psychological organization. Transactive memory also is activated while the partners talk about the meaning and importance of the noted similarity. As a product of talking about the noted similarity partners may encode the discussed commonality into their relational schemata in similar fashions—they may interactively experience it in parallel form. When this occurs it facilitates understanding of the way the partner thinks, and understanding the thought processes of one's partner is an important step toward connecting with that person (Kelly, 1969).

Up to this point I have examined the effects of actual similarity in relationships, and the role played by communication in moderating those effects. Of equal (and perhaps greater) importance is the impact of perceived and/or assumed similarity. Investigations have revealed that individuals perceive more similarity between their attitudes and those of their partner than actually exists, a process referred to as assimilation (Sillars & Scott, 1983,

p. 155). In some circumstances perceived similarity has a greater impact on relational dynamics than does actual similarity (Acitelli, Douvan, & Veroff, 1993; Monsour, Betty, & Kurzweil, 1993). Whereas perceived similarity implies the existence of some kind of perceptual process that acts as the basis for the perception, assumed similarity suggests that similarity is taken for granted or imagined, rather than being the product of some specific perceptual process.

Understanding in Relationships

Now let us examine the role of understanding in the development of intimacy in a relationship, and the connection of understanding to the communication of dis/similarities. Kelly (1969) contends that there are two levels of understanding another person. At one level, P observes O's behavior and construes that behavior from P's perspective. At a second level of understanding P attempts to interpret O's behavior in the same way O would. Similar to Kelly's first level of understanding is the position that understanding exists when P accurately knows the attitude or belief of his or her partner toward some X (Acitelli, 1993; White, 1985). These views of understanding are limited in that they do not entail individual and/or mutual realization of mis/understanding: Individuals may be in/accurate in their understanding of one another's views toward X, but may not realize that in/accuracy exists (Laing et al., 1966).

Communicating about dis/similarity can have a broad range of effects on the level of understanding in a relationship, just as the degree of understanding in a relationship might influence what dis/similarities are communicated. The effects of communicating about dis/similarity on understanding are contingent on such factors as whether or not individuals want to understand and be understood by their partner, the competency level of each partner, and the types of dis/similarities being communicated. When an individual does not wish to be understood by a relational partner he or she may engage in equivocation or outright deception. In a similar vein, attempting to understand a relational partner who is equivocating or lying could be an immensely frustrating experience, particularly when understanding is crucial to making competent relational choices. From a competency perspective, if one communicates an important dis/similarity but that communication is misunderstood, then the interaction and even the relationship may take a decidedly different trajectory. By the same token, if an individual does not understand the meaning of a communicated dis/similarity, perhaps because it was obscured by equivocation or because the individual is hearing what he or she wants to hear, that individual may react to the information in an unwarranted fashion. Finally, the type of dis/similarity that is communicated can determine the effect it will have on understanding. For example, communicating about dis/similar opinions or things external to the relationship would have less of an impact on level of relational understanding than would communication about dis/similar values and things internal to the relationship.

In the serial construction of meaning (Duck, 1994a), understanding takes on broader ramifications. It entails not only P accurately knowing O's view on specific Xs, but also the accurate extension of knowledge of a specific similarity to other areas. Extensions facilitate an integrated understanding of the whole individual and how he or she thinks. The meanings attached by partners to specific and extended similarities, and the extent to which partners similarly construct the meaning of experiences (Kelly, 1970), both influence understanding. Of course the possibility exists that the extension of some dis/similarities to other areas may be unjustified, and would lead to a misunderstanding of one's partner and a false sense of dis/similarity. Accurate understanding of the similarities and differences between oneself and a relational partner lays the groundwork for building intimacy in a relationship.

Intimacy in Relationships

Though there is general agreement among those who study personal relationships that intimacy is a pivotal construct, there is considerably less agreement on the meaning of intimacy (Perlman & Fehr, 1987; Register & Henley, 1992). Nevertheless, several commentators have conceptualized intimacy in ways that allow for direct links to the ideas thus far explicated. For example, Erikson (1963) contends that real intimacy is possible only after an individual has developed a sense of identity. An extrapolation from Erikson's basic contention allows for the establishment of a connection between similarity, sense of identity, and intimacy in a relationship. When a partner has the same attitudes or values as oneself, those similarities help to confirm the validity of one's own attitudes and values (Duck, 1976). In a similar vein, when partners reveal dissimilarities it may have the positive consequences of making both individuals feel unique (Wood, Dendy, Dordek, Germany, & Varallo, in press). Consequently, the communication of dis/similarities can play an important role in a person's quest for establishing a sense of identity, thereby paving the way for building intimacy in a relationship.

A recent phenomenological perspective on intimacy helps to elucidate the connection between similarity of minds and the development of intimacy. Register and Henley (1992) asked subjects to recall and describe an experience that they would consider to be intimate. In the analysis of the accounts of the subjects three themes presented themselves that are relevant to this chapter. All three themes reflect a conceptualization of intimacy as a process that is mutually constructed, requiring substantial relational work. The presence theme is one in which individuals report that they feel the presence of their partner, even though he or she may not be physically present. To the extent that relational partners understand the thought processes of one another—particularly as they relate to noted areas of dis/similarities—those partners might feel one another's presence. For example, if P is at a movie that she knows her absent partner would like because they have similar tastes in movies, she may think of her partner during the movie and actually feel his or her presence.

Two other themes uncovered by Register and Henley that have relevance to this analysis are boundary and transformation. With

the boundary theme respondents reported that they felt as
though boundaries between themselves and their partner were
removed, leading to getting inside the "life world" of the other
individual (Register & Henley, 1992, p. 474). The transformation
theme is one in which partners feel as though something new
has been created through the process of getting to know one another. Both themes are related to the process of constructing a
symbolic union between partners, and the concept of dyadic
intersubjectivity, which is the similarity of thought-feeling content that develops in a dyad as a consequence of their interaction
(Ickes et al., 1988).

Conclusions

A number of conclusions can be drawn from the various literatures examined in this chapter, conclusions that suggest future
directions of exploration in the study of relationship processes.
Recall that the primary goal of this chapter was to determine
the effects of communicating about dis/similarity, and to ascertain how such communication (competent and incompetent)
might influence the development of understanding and intimacy
in a relationship. To draw conclusions concerning the effects of
communicating about dis/similarity it was necessary to delineate
the similarity construct.

The first conclusion of this chapter is that conceptualizations
of similarity have been limited in that they have viewed similarity
as a state, rather than a process; as having absolute effects, rather
than contingent ones; and as being a unidimensional construct,
rather than a multidimensional one. Similarity between relational partners should be viewed as an ongoing dyadic process of
discovery, disclosure, and mutual construction entailing both
cognitive and interactional competencies. The similarity construct needs to be expanded to encompass a number of processes that have been underemphasized or ignored. Duck's pioneering work in this area, most clearly illustrated by his model of the

serial construction of meaning, could be used as a point of departure for investigating some of those processes.

As noted by Duck (1994a), his model can be interpreted and extended to cover a wide range of processes inherent in the ongoing construction of meaning in a relationship. For example, one might construe the model in ways that allow for the construction of similarities, as well as the mutual and individual negotiation of dissimilarities. In a process model of similarity construction partners would become more similar, and the establishment of those similarities would take place at both the dyadic and the individual levels.

A number of constructs discussed in this chapter would be operative in the construction of similarities, but those most central would be mutual knowledge and transactive memory (Planalp & Garvin-Doxas, Chapter 1 in this volume; Wegner et al., 1985), dyadic intersubjectivity (Ickes et al., 1988), relational talk and awareness (Acitelli, 1993), transformation (Register & Henley, 1992), assimilation (Sillars & Scott, 1983), and extension (Duck, 1994a). Take the example of two individuals, P and O, contemplating their impending marriage. P and O each have a store of mutual knowledge, which is knowledge that the two partners share, know they share, and use during interaction with one another (Planalp & Garvin-Doxas, Chapter 1 in this volume). Mutual knowledge includes knowledge of dis/similarities, and is stored in a transactive memory structure, which is one memory unit shared by both partners (Wegner et al., 1985). Each time P and O engage in relational talk (Acitelli, 1993) about their feelings for one another and their attitudes toward marriage they draw on mutual knowledge of their dis/similarities in an attempt to discover and create common ground in their understanding of marriage. Progressively over a period of months (or days, or even hours) P and O may take one important similarity, such as the fact that they each want to marry the other, and through semantic elaboration (Anderson & Reder, 1979), extension (Duck, 1994a), and dyadic intersubjectivity (Ickes et al., 1988), that similarity acts as the basis for the construction of other similarities crucial to establishing a common perceptual view of marriage.

This might include views on in-laws, children, friends, sex, intimacy, religion, marital roles, and anything else that might have bearing on their marital relationship. In a real sense their relationship is transformed (Register & Henley, 1992) through multiple cognitive and interactional processes. For instance, if P and O discover through declaration (Duck, 1994a) that they both have read Gibran's (1923) *The Prophet,* and that they each agree with him that in marriage there should be "spaces in your togetherness" (p. 15), that discovery of similarity helps to establish and define intimacy in their relationship. Based on that similarity they may further agree that they each believe they should have their own friends, their own religion, and a certain degree of independence. Though some of the constructed and extended similarities may be a result of assimilation (Sillars & Scott, 1983) to the extent that the various processes are engendered competently through talk, the partners can avoid assuming similarity where there is none.

Equally important as the communication and construction of similarities is the intentional and unintentional communication of dissimilarities. What role does the realization of fundamental dissimilarity play in the development of intimacy and understanding in a relationship? More central to our concerns, how are dissimilarities between relational partners reconciled (negotiated) and integrated through talk into a coherent whole that we conveniently label "the relationship"? Some argue that dissimilarities between relational partners, even fundamental ones, need not damage the relationship (Byrne & Lamberth, 1971; Wood et al., in press). Dissimilarities do not have absolute effects on a relationship, rather it is the meaning assigned to those dissimilarities that determines whether they will help or hinder relational growth (Byrne & Lamberth, 1971). As observed by Wood and associates (in press), noted and accepted dissimilarities in a relationship can be taken as evidence by the relational partners that they accept one another for who they are, which in turn brings them closer together, rather than pulling them further apart. Though Duck's model does not explicitly concern itself with persuasive processes, persuasion between partners undoubtedly would play a large role in the mutual construction of similarities as partners attempt to convert differences into commonalities. For instance, if two individuals contemplating marriage disagree as to whether or not to have children, the reconciliation of that dissimilarity, whether through persuasion or some other means, is certainly crucial to understanding, intimacy, and the joint construction of meaning.

A second conclusion of this chapter concerns the pivotal importance of talk in the realization of understanding and dis/similarity in a relationship. In the talk that occurs between relational partners a number of stumbling blocks present themselves that make mutual understanding a sometimes arduous undertaking. As reviewed, these stumbling blocks include, but are not limited to, equivocation and politeness. This chapter did not examine the equally perilous obstacles of deception and ingratiation (Knapp & Comadena, 1979; Neuberg, Judice, Virdin, & Carrillo, 1993). The employment of communication strategies such as equivocation, politeness, deception, and ingratiation may lead to a false sense of dis/similarity. Future research endeavors should examine the integration of cognitive and interactional competencies that are invoked during talk in a relationship, and how those processes combine to establish mutuality of meaning in a relationship.

A third conclusion of this chapter concerns the effects of communicating about dis/similarity on understanding and intimacy in a relationship. Although this may be an oversimplification, the competent communication of information about oneself, as well as the competent gleaning of information about one's partner, should facilitate a sharing of meaning and understanding in a relationship. The competent communication and gathering of information involve a plethora of related processes such as equivocation, extension, semantic elaboration, transformation, empathic communication and accuracy, second-guessing, and dyadic intersubjectivity. These processes impact the level of understanding and influence intimacy between partners.

A final conclusion of this chapter is that only a small part of the relational process puzzle has been presented. There is so much going on during interaction that to narrowly focus on the effects of communicating about dis/similarity would be a clear oversimplification. Though the linking and integration of relational partners through cognitive and interactional processes are indeed important, of equal importance are other variables examined throughout this series on understanding relationship processes. For example, how do the processes explicated in this chapter operate in relationships conducted over electronic systems (Lea & Spears, in press), or in long-distance relationships (Rohlfing, in press), or in relationships between enemies in which similarities may be discounted and dissimilarities amplified (Wiseman, in press)? What impact do third parties have on how relational partners view and incorporate dis/similarities into their joint construction of the relationship (Klein & Milardo, 1993)? In the enormous complexities of relational life, an examination of as many relational processes as possible must be tempered with the realization that the whole will always be greater than the sum of its parts.

Nonverbal Behavior in Dyadic Interactions

Maureen P. Keeley

Allen J. Hart

The quality of a personal relationship is inexorably related to the quality of communication between the parties involved in that relationship. In fact, relationships often are evaluated in terms of their subjectively perceived quality (Montgomery, 1988). The assessment of the quality of the relationship is based largely on aspects of the communication process (e.g., frequency, satisfaction). Indeed, since the 1960s communication has been regarded as the key to improving a relationship.

The present chapter focuses on the role of nonverbal behavior in the assessment of the quality of personal relationships. Relationship quality is the gauge by which personal relationships are judged. Communication, both verbal and nonverbal, is inherent in that assessment. We argue in this chapter that nonverbal communication plays an underestimated role in quality of communication and also in the quality of relationships. In so doing we show how nonverbal communication is the foundation of much that is essential to the dynamics of relationships and the assessments of those relationships.

The chapter integrates the research literatures on functional approaches to understanding nonverbal communication and quality communication. We claim that judgments about relationship quality are linked to the functions of nonverbal communication that heretofore have been underestimated in the dynamics of relationships. After defining what we mean by nonverbal communication, especially the dynamic cues attended to during face-to-face interactions, we outline three dimensions by which the quality of communication is evaluated in a relationship. We then argue that nonverbal communication is essential to establishing and maintaining quality communication in personal relationships. Similarly, nonverbal communication patterns may indicate a decrease in relationship quality that is often present during the deescalation stage in a relationship. This chapter thus contributes to the volume by examining the functions of nonverbal communication, rather than specific cues, to increase our understanding of what makes relationships satisfying.

We begin with a definition of nonverbal communication. At its most informal level, nonverbal communication means all the messages (i.e., meaning-laden information) that people exchange other than words. More formally, nonverbal communication refers to signs and symbols (both static and dynamic) that qualify as potential messages by virtue of their regular and consistent use and interpretation. The nonverbal rules and practices of a culture are organized into codes. Codes are organized message systems consisting of a set of symbols and the rules for their use. For the purposes of this chapter we define the nonverbal codes by their means of expression. Each code is communicated by a different part of the nonverbal world: a part of the body, the environment, or objects. We emphasize the dynamic nonverbal codes, those that may potentially change during an interaction: *kinesics,* body movement or body language in the vernacular, including eye behavior; vocal activity or *vocalics*; *haptics* or touching behavior; and *proxemics* or the use of space. These are best described as the performance and spatial codes; that is, those executed by the human body—body movement, facial expression, eye gaze, touch, vocal activity, and personal space. The static codes, *artifacts* (i.e., the use of materials and objects to communicate), *physical appearance* (e.g., attractiveness, race, gender, clothing), *chronemics* (i.e., the use of time), and *olfactics* (i.e., the use of smell) are not focused on in this chapter (DeVito & Hecht, 1990). It is also important to note that cues get their specific meanings based on the particular situation, past experiences, and the knowledge of the partner in the interaction. In other words, depending on the context, the same cues may have different meaning or different cues may have the same meaning. In sum, we consider all performance and spatial behaviors that are intentionally performed, are used with regularity, and have consensual meaning to be nonverbal communication.

We concentrate on the nonverbal codes that communicate messages actively during an interaction for two reasons. First, the dynamic cues are an integral part of the communication, whereas the static cues have an impact but are part of the larger environment in which the message is communicated. Second, the dynamic cues directly impact the relationship because they often are monitored vigilantly during an interaction, especially during times of relational conflict or change. We argue that it is these more dynamic nonverbal codes that greatly affect quality communication and ultimately the quality of the personal relationship itself.

Quality Communication

Montgomery's (1988) investigation into what composes good communication in relationships focused on three standards: the ideals of positivity, intimacy, and control. Her discussion suggested that the assessments of these three criteria are highly dependent on nonverbal symbols. Specifically, she stated that "valenced (positive or negative) nonverbal behaviors are more strongly related to quality than valenced verbal behaviors"

(p. 345). Intimacy is created not only through verbal, but also through nonverbal, revealing, expressing, and sharing between two people in a relationship. Last, control of the relationship often is communicated through the management of interactions through coordinated nonverbal behaviors. This suggests that nonverbal communication plays a critical, and perhaps underestimated, role in establishing and maintaining the quality communication in personal relationships. By way of understanding interpersonal relationship dynamics, this chapter discusses the usefulness of nonverbal communication, and the functions that nonverbal behaviors serve to affect the quality of communication in dyadic relationships.

The quality of everyday interaction is the litmus test of personal relationships (e.g., romantic, friendship, parent-child) and ultimately defines the relationship (Montgomery, 1988). Good and bad patterns of communication are associated with good and bad relationships, respectively. More specifically, "good communication is deemed to be that which is positively related to the happiness and satisfaction that partners experience in their relationship" (Montgomery, 1988, p. 344). The quality of communication is evaluated most often along the dimensions of positivity, intimacy, and control.

The Ideal of Positivity

The concept of positivity is pervasive in our society and in the study of personal relationships. Individuals are taught from a very young age to say nice or positive things about others or to not say anything at all (Montgomery, 1988). Similarly, relational scholars have spent the majority of their efforts examining positive topics (e.g., intimacy, love, romance, support, facilitation of relationships, etc.) (Duck, 1994b). To highlight the importance of positivity in the interaction process, Montgomery (1988) identifies two aspects of the ideal of positivity.

First, positivity refers to how the exchange of positive and negative behaviors relates to quality. Relationships are created, maintained, and dissolved through the interaction process; therefore, the degree of positivity exchanged between the dyadic members during the interaction may distinguish between functional and dysfunctional relationships. Research focusing on dynamic exchanges has found that it is more important to avoid exchanging negative patterns of interaction than it is to reciprocate positive patterns of interaction (Gottman, 1991; Gottman & Krokoff, 1989). Pike and Sillars (1985) found that nonverbal affective patterns (especially negative affect) have more relational meaning than does verbal disclosure. Further, negative behaviors are more likely to be reciprocated in dysfunctional relationships (Pike & Sillars, 1985). Clearly the assessment of positive and negative affect impacts dyadic interactions; such impact often is created by nonverbal means.

The second aspect of positivity noted by Montgomery involves the communication of relational expressions of positivity (Montgomery, 1988). Relational expressions of positivity are created over time through patterns of behaviors, rather than any one behavior. More specifically, relational expressions focus on interaction patterns that serve to confirm each partner as an individual or to confirm each of their roles in the relationship. Positivity also can be expressed as awareness of a partner's value in the relationship and endorsement of the emotional experiences of each other (Cissna & Sieburg, 1981). Duck (1994b) concurs, stating that "relational acts are positive when they impinge upon the meanings that a person has for the relationship and the partner in a positive way, and negative when they affect those images negatively" (p. 33).

The Ideal of Intimacy

During the past two decades intimacy has been perceived to be the desired goal of personal relationships. Intimacy is not a quality of persons alone, nor inherent in any relationship, but is forged through the interaction process (Reis & Shaver, 1988). Intimacy is achieved through communication, through the sharing of verbal and nonverbal symbols that reveal two people to each other. Davis (1973) asserts that for two individuals to become intimate, they must establish "continued encounters on a regular basis" (p. 30). This perspective underscores that it is only through the process of interaction that intimacy is created and maintained. High levels of intimacy are associated with good relationships in this society and in scholarly reports. Montgomery (1988) identifies five criteria associated with the ideal of intimacy and the communication process.

First, Montgomery (1988) maintains that relationship quality is more closely associated with the nonverbal channel of expression than it is with the verbal channel. Why is this so? Perhaps it is because much of our meaning in interpersonal exchanges is derived from nonverbal channels (Burgoon, 1985). In addition, nonverbal behaviors are viewed as being more spontaneous and honest (Burgoon, Buller, & Woodall, 1989), which corresponds easily with the view that intimacy is not created from a strategic plan, but instead from dynamic behaviors (some of them nonverbal).

Second, the expressions of intimacy and quality communication in personal relationships vary over time. Personal relationships cycle between openness and closedness based on the interactants' needs for togetherness and autonomy (Altman et al., 1981). The issue of cycling and patterns of intimacy emphasizes, as does this volume, the dynamic nature of dyadic interactions.

Third, partners do not necessarily contribute equally in the communication of intimacy (Montgomery, 1988). Women tend to communicate more intimacy in their relationships and tend to value intimacy in their relationships more than do men (Dosser, Balswick, & Halverson, 1986). In romantic relationships females are better at providing intimacy than males and have more intimate interactions than males (Reis, Senchak, & Soloman, 1985). In addition, females are more intimate and emotional in their same-sex friendships than males (Aukett, Ritchie, & Mill, 1988). Thus the difference in each partner's sense of the relative imbalance with regard to their own contribution toward intimacy also may affect their view of the intimacy of the relationship.

Fourth, expressive messages can be positive or negative, and the quality of communication corresponds directly with the interpretation and degree of positivity (Montgomery, 1988). The research has focused on the effects of negative messages. Negative messages are associated with poor or troubled relationships. Negative messages also are associated with inconsistent information. Planalp and Honeycutt (1985) found that new information that is inconsistent with known or expected information from friends or romantic partners increased levels of uncertainty, and often led to decreases in the quality of their relationships. To the extent that men and women differ in nonverbal communication expressiveness, we would expect to find gender-related differences in assessment of quality. This is consistent with Noller's (1984) findings that husbands and wives in unhappy marriages differed in their assessments of relationship quality.

Fifth, the way that intimacy is expressed is as important as whether intimacy is expressed at all (Montgomery, 1988). The degree of responsiveness that is displayed through nonverbal behavior is vital to the expression of intimacy between close friends and marital partners (Berg, 1987). The omission of unpleasant or nonintimate behavior in dyadic interactions also may be viewed by the interactants as an expression of intimacy in personal relationships (Knapp, 1983). In addition, it is important that the level of intimacy expressed through verbal and nonverbal behaviors remains consistent. If there is a discrepancy between verbal and nonverbal channels, nonverbal channels are focused on more often and believed. Specifically, people rely most heavily on visual cues, less on vocal cues, and the least amount on verbal cues to decipher mixed messages (Mehrabian & Ferris, 1967). In fact, Mehrabian (1981) found that we evaluate persons themselves on the basis of their nonverbal cues and persons' acts on the basis of their verbal behavior.

The Ideal of Control

The ideal of control focuses on people's desire to direct or be in control of their relationships (Montgomery, 1988). Individuals like to feel that they have control over the destiny of their relationships. Quality relationships, therefore, are the result of hard work, effort, and a desire on the part of the interactants to make them work (Katriel & Philipsen, 1981). Montgomery identifies a number of elements critical to the perception of control in relationships. In the first place, to exercise control in a relationship, partners must be able to make predictions about the future of that relationship and be able to affect those future happenings. Just as importantly, though, interactants must be able to manage their communication and not feel that their interactions rule their relationships.

The ideal of control also focuses on specific kinds of interactional patterns. For instance, both partners must feel that their own nonverbal behaviors are synchronized and coordinated with those of their partners. Further, partners preoccupied with meta-communication (i.e., talking about their communication patterns) often feel as though they have lost some control over the interaction. Gottman (1991) found that individuals in dysfunctional relationships tend to fixate on the meta-communication rather than on the source of the conflict itself.

Shared meaning is the last element described by Montgomery (1988) as being relevant to the ideal of control and quality communication in personal relationships. Shared meaning in relationships is derived from both verbal and nonverbal symbols. Sillars and Scott (1983) found that dissatisfied marital partners disagreed more with each other regarding the interpretation of messages than did satisfied partners. Further, Noller and Venardos (1986) stress that dissatisfied partners also assume that their interpretations of the interactions are correct more often than do satisfied couples. Unfortunately, the more confident individuals are about their perceptions, the more accurate their perceptions appear to others, when in fact there is little or no relationship between confidence and accuracy. So in addition to dissatisfied couples having less shared meaning, the individual partners are more confident that their own perceptions are right compared to the confidence in perceptions of satisfied partners.

The standards of positivity, intimacy, and control for examining quality communication in personal relationships offer a novel way to examine how and why nonverbal symbols impact and influence dyadic interactions in personal relationships. Closer inspection of these components of quality communication in terms of specific elements of nonverbal communication should provide us with the tools to inspect the overall role and impact of nonverbal communication in dyadic interactions. Examination of nonverbal symbols in dyadic interactions often is organized by nonverbal codes (e.g., kinesics, vocalics, haptics, proxemics, chronemics, physical appearance, artifacts/environment, and olfactics). Yet this method of organization and research leads to oversimplification and increases the risk of looking at only one channel at a time. Multiple cues from multiple channels influence dyadic interactions in personal relationships; consequently, this simplified classification system based on separate codes is inadequate. We are especially concerned that the risk of oversimplification is prevalent in analyses and speculations about the dynamics of ongoing relationships. Researchers may be most confident about the role of nonverbal communication in precisely those contexts in which we know the least about their actual complexities.

Classifying nonverbal behaviors in terms of the functions that they perform during interactions might prove to be more ecologically valid, realistic, and useful. Functions are the motives, objectives, or consequences of communication (Burgoon et al., 1989). Patterson (1992) stresses that behaviors are organized and interdependent. Therefore, examining multiple cues in multiple channels from a functional perspective will reflect more accurately the process during dynamic interactions in personal relationships.

Nonverbal Functional Approach
to Relational Dynamics

Functional analysis of nonverbal behavior focuses on constellations of nonverbal cues and emphasizes patterns of nonverbal interactions for specific purposes in relationships (Burgoon et al., 1989; Patterson, 1992). Interactants' behaviors that make up the patterns of interactions are guided by the perceived purposes of the interaction (Patterson, 1992). These perceptions can be conscious or not, depending on the situation and relationship. Regardless of the level of awareness, people enter interactions with habitual ways of behaving toward others because of their behavioral predispositions, arousal level, and cognitive-affective reactions (Patterson, 1992). Interactants' habitual patterns of behavior should be similar in nature for any specific function. There are at least eight distinct functions of nonverbal behaviors: (a) information and identification; (b) impression formation and management; (c) affect management; (d) relational intimacy, involvement, and dominance; (e) managing interaction; (f) mixed messages and deception; (g) social influence; and (h) message production, processing, and comprehension. These different functions communicate messages about the individual, and perhaps more importantly for the purposes of this chapter, about the couple as a couple. Our discussion concentrates on the dynamic interaction between the interactants but also addresses how couples are perceived by others. Explanation of these functions, discussion of the nonverbal cues exhibited during the communication of these functions, and examination of their role in quality communication should increase our understanding of the impact of nonverbal communication during dyadic interactions.

Of the functional analyses advanced by researchers, those by Burgoon (1980, 1985; Burgoon et al., 1989) and Patterson (1982, 1983, 1987, 1992) are the most comprehensive and are very similar in nature. Burgoon's perspective focuses on nonverbal cues (i.e., cues that communicate specific messages), whereas Patterson's classification focuses specifically on nonverbal presentation (i.e., perceptions manifested through nonverbal cues). These two classification systems combine insights regarding dyadic interactions from both the communication and social-psychological perspectives of personal relationships. Because of their resemblances and their compatible perspectives, a combination of the two classification approaches can be used for exploring the impact of nonverbal behaviors on "quality communication." Research examining dyadic interactions in personal relationships that provides support for each function of nonverbal communication also is explored in terms of the three ideals of quality communication.

Informational Function and Identification

Nonverbal behaviors provide information from which observers can make attributions concerning an individual's traits, motivations, or states (Patterson, 1992). Burgoon and associates (1989) concur that nonverbal behaviors provide information, but add that nonverbal cues project self-identities through cues revealing an individual's personality, goals, and feelings. Nonverbal cues also identify a couple as a couple. Thus not only does the information allow others to make attributions, but it also allows interactants to intentionally communicate a clear and unambiguous message about who they are and how others are to interact with them.

Positivity

The positive and negative expression of basic emotions is universally communicated through facial expressions and provides information about the states or motivations of the interactants (Ekman, Friesen, & Ancoli, 1980). Nonverbal behaviors also are informative in that they may tell the individual expressing the negative or positive affect about his or her own feelings or reactions (Tomkins, 1981). These two simple examples serve to illustrate how nonverbal behaviors provide information about the positive and negative affects that occur during all dyadic interactions. The function of providing information is a pervasive one during exchanges, and because individuals can and do make judgments of negative and positive affect from nonverbal cues, the ideal of positivity is an important one for relationships.

The issue of positivity is also important given information about personality, gender, culture, and race. For instance, individuals whose nonverbal behaviors communicate domineering, pushy, or shy personalities often are judged more negatively than individuals whose nonverbal behaviors indicate that they are giving, helpful, outgoing, or happy. Judgments about personality have been confirmed by research examining parents' evaluations of children based on body types (Walker, 1963) and by research based on interactants' positive and negative judgments concerning the voice (Markel, Phillis, Vargas, & Howard, 1972). Individuals also make negative or positive judgments based on such nonverbal cues as the distance that is kept during interactions (Morris, 1977), or the amount of eye contact during interactions (Byers & Byers, 1972). These perceptions often become self-fulfilling prophecies during dyadic interactions in that the interactant may behave in a way that is consistent with the perceptions obtained from the interaction.

Information of this nature has its greatest impact during the earliest stages of a relationship. Once relationships develop there is less of a need to make judgments based on the identification of personality, gender, culture, or race. Interactants then will rely more heavily on the information based on past experiences, as well as the motivations and current state of their partners.

Intimacy

During the escalation period of friendship and romantic relationship development, the function of gender identification is important. Males and females differ in how they perceive and communicate intimacy in relationships (Reis et al., 1985). Women tend to convey more intimacy in their relationships than do men (Dosser et al., 1986). Thus based on the gender of the dyads (e.g., male-male, male-female, female-female), nonverbal cues communicating intimacy will differ during all stages of relational development, but especially during the initiating, experimenting, and intensifying stages. In addition, intimacy is generated and preserved through interactions (Davis, 1973). Therefore, the information communicated between the interactants about their motivations and mood through nonverbal cues impacts the ideal of intimacy continually throughout dyadic interactions.

Control

Information is control. Nonverbal behaviors give interactants information about their partners' moods, traits, and motivations through all eight nonverbal codes, but especially through facial expressions (Ekman et al., 1980). An increase in information often leads to a decrease in uncertainty and an increase in control (Berger & Calabrese, 1975). Nonverbal cues contribute a significant amount to the overall information communicated during dyadic interactions, and therefore are critical to the ideal of control in relationships and quality communication.

Impression Formation and Management

Nonverbal behaviors are used to display or augment an image at the individual level or to create an identity for the couple (Patterson, 1992), and as such they serve a self-presentational function for both the individual partners and the couple. This function highlights the importance of nonverbal symbols for the creation and management of personal and joint impressions. On the other hand, Burgoon and associates' (1989) perspective on impression formation and management emphasizes that nonverbal cues are used to nurture and manipulate certain impressions throughout the relationship. The difference lies in the target at which the nonverbal communication is aimed: Patterson (1992) sees the presentational patterns as being "designed to influence third-party observers and not the immediate-interaction partner" (p. 480); Burgoon feels that the focus is on the interacting members of the dyad. Both perspectives pertain to how and why individuals communicate images and impressions during dyadic interactions, and both are explored here in greater detail; after all, many dyadic exchanges occur in the presence of an audience.

The key to understanding the function of the creation and management of impressions is the understanding that people make a wide range of judgments based on a limited amount of information derived primarily from nonverbal channels. Impressions are comprised of physical, sociocultural, and psychological judgments (Burgoon et al., 1989). First impressions are important because they provide a baseline of comparison for all future interactions. The management of impressions remains important through all stages of relational development, but especially so during relationship dissolution because of the need to form alliances and to save face with one's network (Duck, 1982). Impression management (to partner and to outside audience) can be more closely explored through discussion of its impact on the judgment of quality communication in terms of positivity, intimacy, and control.

Positivity

From a very young age individuals are told to make a good first impression when meeting someone by smiling, having a firm handshake, making eye contact, looking nice, and so on. These rudimentary suggestions are made because it is generally acknowledged that first impressions are influenced by outward appearances and behavior during initial interactions (Burgoon, 1985). People who do not make extended eye contact, keep their distance from others, do not smile, and/or have a weak handshake often are described as being antisocial, strange, or weak. Individuals who smile often, have pleasant facial expressions, and have pleasant vocal qualities are perceived as more likeable, exciting, strong, and poised. People who are viewed positively are judged more physically attractive and tend to have more satisfying interactions (Duck, 1988). The previous negative connotations are based on first impressions (often made within the first 30 seconds of the interaction) created from nonverbal cues.

The management of positive and negative impressions continues throughout relationships. Interactants are acutely aware of the positive and negative impacts of nonverbal behavior for managing impressions especially during deescalation of relationships. Interactants communicate to each other their dissatisfaction with the relationship through changing nonverbal cues such as decreases in physical proximity, decreases in the rate and duration of touch, and decreases in smiling and mutual looks (Miller & Parks, 1982).

Interactants also present positive and negative messages to third-party observers (Patterson, 1987). Close attention to one's partner through extended eye gaze, holding hands, public kisses, and the like communicates to others that the couple has a strong, loving, and positive relationship. On the other hand, couples who are breaking up often present negative impressions about their relationship to people in their network (e.g., decreased touching, decreased frequency and duration of eye gaze) (Miller & Parks, 1982). This signals to the partner and to the network that the relationship is in distress.

Intimacy

The nonverbal function of impression management is important for the ideal of intimacy because interactants often communicate their willingness to become intimate through nonverbal cues. Presentation of cues that signal openness, affiliativeness, warmth, and immediacy indicate that individuals are attracted to others (Mehrabian, 1981). Some of the nonverbal cues that signal attraction during relationship development include congruent body positions, interactional synchrony, warm and soft tonal qualities, extended eye gaze, and smiles (Burgoon, Buller, Hale, & deTurck, 1984). These patterns should reverse during stages of dissolution (Miller & Parks, 1982), allowing partners to manage their impressions so as to reduce intimacy.

Control

The ideal of control on quality communication can be applied to the presentational function. One way that interactants may create a sense that they have control over their relationship is to concoct an identity or image for others observing the relationship. For instance, romantic partners wanting outsiders to recognize and confirm their relationship may nonverbally express their closeness and commitment by holding each other's gaze, maintaining direct body orientation, holding hands, standing close, and being very expressive (Patterson, 1987). Managing impressions within the dyadic interaction (between parent and child, for instance) is associated with responsiveness, synchrony, and predictability of nonverbal behaviors (Condon & Sander, 1974).

Affect Management

Managing affect is the softening or modulating of emotions in order to regulate the consequences of emotional displays (Patterson, 1992). However, the perception of nonverbal cues as merely softening emotions is rather limiting. Nonverbal behaviors also are acknowledged as the fundamental way that individuals express intentional emotions and cathartic (often unintentional) displays of emotion (Burgoon et al., 1989).

Positivity

Additional proof that the ideal of positivity remains strong in our society is reflected in the social acceptance of the portrayal of negative and positive emotions between interactants. Embarrassment, fear, anger, sadness, and social anxiety (as portrayed through tears, reduced eye contact, reduced body orientation, and even increased distance between interactants) are associated with high levels of public self-consciousness (Patterson, 1987). The nonverbal display of these negative emotions is discouraged, forcing interactants to manage these affects to limit the vulnerability of the individuals experiencing the emotions (Patterson, 1987). At the other end of the emotion spectrum are positive emotions such as joy, pleasant surprise, and exhilaration, as displayed through laughter, hugs, kisses, shared smiling, and even "high-fives." These positive affect displays are considered more acceptable for public dyadic interactions than negative affect displays, and therefore are displayed more often in public. The display of nonverbal cues signaling positive and negative emotions between partners in personal relationships is constrained by gender, age, cultural norms, and personality characteristics (e.g., externalizers versus internalizers) of the interactants (Burgoon et al., 1989).

The ideal of positivity in quality communication is especially relevant for married couples. Specifically, negative patterns of affect that are displayed primarily through nonverbal behaviors (e.g., rolling of eyes, facial expressions of disgust and contempt, physically pulling away) are important indicators of marital dissatisfaction. Research focusing on conflict exchanges found that it is more important to avoid exchanging the aforementioned negative patterns of interaction than it is to reciprocate positive interaction patterns, such as head nods, increased eye gaze, smiling, and touching (Gottman, 1991; Gottman & Krokoff, 1989). Levenson and Gottman (1983, 1985) found that interactions between distressed marital partners contained more negative affect and more reciprocity of negative affect than did nondistressed couples' interactions. Gottman, Markman, and Notarius (1977) similarly found that dissatisfied couples were involved in more negative cycles of affect than were satisfied couples. For instance, when one marital partner speaks in a raised voice with a negative tone, the other partner responds in kind.

Intimacy

Nonverbal signals are especially important for conveying affective information that is critical to the establishment and maintenance of intimate relationships (Walker & Trimboli, 1989). "Looking, laughing, and smiling are powerful nonverbal signals of warmth and attentiveness in interpersonal relationships" (McAdams, Jackson, & Kirshnit, 1984, p. 261). These positive expressions of nonverbal affect are associated with people who have a high need for intimacy (McAdams et al., 1984). These behaviors also are manifested in situations in which the dyadic members of the interaction feel liking, loving, happiness, or attraction toward one another (McAdams et al., 1984).

Control

The idea of control and the concept of emotional expressions are closely linked because of interactants' need to have some predictability regarding the future of their relationships. First, predictability is associated with decoding accuracy of emotional expressions. For instance, wives' ability to accurately decode their husbands' expressions (especially negative affect) correlates with the wives' marital complaints (Sabatelli, Buck, & Kenny, 1986). Second, different patterns of emotional expressions can predict marital satisfaction over time. Gottman and Krokoff (1989) found that negative emotional patterns of communication (defensiveness, stubbornness, and withdrawal), which often are communicated nonverbally by marital partners, are dysfunctional for marriages longitudinally and predictive of relationship dissolution.

Relational Intimacy, Involvement, and Dominance

Nonverbal involvement is a function of relational intimacy and openness. Generally speaking, the greater the degree of intimacy in a relationship, the greater the level of openness between the interactants, the stronger the union between the pair, and the greater the degree of nonverbal involvement (Patterson, 1992). Nonverbal involvement acts as an indicator of the intimacy level between partners (Patterson, 1992). In addition to communicating intimacy, nonverbal cues also signal the partners' definitions of the relationship in terms of the involvement and dominance levels (Burgoon et al., 1989). These nonverbal cues differ depending on the type of relationship (e.g., parent-child, friendship, romantic) and the stage of the relationship (e.g., relational escalation, maintenance, or dissolution).

Intimacy, involvement, and dominance represent higher-order categories of relational communication. Burgoon and Hale (1984) posit that there may be as many as 12 general themes in relational communication, many of which could not be communicated without the aid of nonverbal cues. The themes include dominance/ submission, emotional arousal, composure, similarity, formality/

informality, task/social, and intimacy (in terms of affection/ hostility, inclusion/exclusion, intensity of involvement, depth/ superficiality, and trust).

Positivity

Intimacy in personal relationships often is seen as something positive. This is perhaps the main reason that individuals seek to increase the level of intimacy in their relationships (Duck & Miell, 1986). Helgeson, Shaver, and Dyer (1987) defined intimacy as feelings and expressions of closeness, appreciation, and affection. This description clearly is based on the ideal of positivity. Expressions of closeness, affection, and involvement also are expressed nonverbally through warm facial expressions, extended eye gaze, mutual smiling, soft touches, and close proximity to one another during interactions. The absence of these nonverbal displays of intimacy is viewed negatively.

The relational messages of dominance, power, and control in personal relationships, on the other hand, are perceived more often as negative elements with respect to quality communication. Nonverbal displays of power in dyadic interactions, such as parents spanking their children at a store, or a couple engaged in a power struggle as evidenced by their mutual threat stare, their facial expressions, and raised voices, often make observers uncomfortable because of the negative nature of these relational messages. All relational messages can be identified on a continuum of positivity based on the context and the members of the dyadic interaction; in fact, this judgment is made all of the time by the interactants and by outside observers of the interaction.

Intimacy

The expression of intimacy is vital to quality communication. Its importance is emphasized by the fact that a primary function of nonverbal behavior is to communicate intimacy (or lack thereof) between interactants in personal relationships. Intimacy often is discussed in terms of romantic relationships, but it is important to highlight the fact that intimacy is also important in friend-ships (Aukett et al., 1988), in parent-child relationships (Cappella, 1991), or in any kind of personal relationship. Keep in mind that intimacy most often is developed and nurtured through con-tinued encounters (Davis, 1973). Support for this recently was found through examination of the attachment and bonding process between mothers and their newborns (Cappella, 1991). Cappella (1991) found that stimulation regulation and emotional respon-siveness were critical to the development of a close and intimate bond between mothers and their babies.

Control

Intimacy is controlled by both interactants: without the will-ing participation of both partners to become intimate, intimacy cannot occur (Reis & Shaver, 1988). In this fashion the expres-sion of intimacy does give interactants relational control. On the other hand, nonverbal behaviors can explicitly signal personal control, dominance, or power by one person over his or her partner during dyadic interactions. These signals shift the balance of relational control in favor of one of the participants over the other. Thus nonverbal cues expressing intimacy can impact rela-tional and personal control.

Managing Interaction

Nonverbal behaviors facilitate the orderly flow of interaction and the degree of involvement that is represented during the interaction (Patterson, 1992). In addition to influencing the sequence and patterning of conversation, nonverbal behaviors also define the situation (Burgoon et al., 1989). The situation is constrained by the structure of the environment, which impacts the dynamics of the interaction. Environmental structure can refer to the physical setting, the rules of behavior consistent with the circumstances, the motivations for the participants in the specific interaction, or the roles that the participants must play given the situation (Furnham & Argyle, 1981).

Positivity

The orderly flow of communication is seen as positive in dyadic interactions and asynchronous conversations are viewed negatively. Warner, Malloy, Schneider, Knoth, and Wilder (1987) found that "increases in rhythmicity or patterning may be associated with increases in positive affect" (p. 62). More specifically, conversations with moderate amounts of rhythm are rated as more positive than conversations with no rhythm or extreme amounts of rhythm (Warner et al., 1987). In addition, individuals who adjust their communication style (e.g., behaviors such as speech rate, eye gaze, number of and duration of smiles) toward their partners are likely to be seen as more attractive than individuals who are not as flexible (Street, 1982).

Intimacy

The importance of interaction patterns on the development of intimate relationships begins at birth and ends only with death. Cappella (1991) states that patterns of interaction "are important to the proper functioning of the psychological and social life of the adult and of the infant. The patterns, when they are disrupted from their normal sequences, may be symptomatic of individual or relational difficulty" (p. 18).

The regulation of mother-child interactions influences the degree of bonding and level of attachment between mothers and their babies. For example, infants whose behaviors were observed to be synchronous with those of their mothers were found to be securely attached at one year of age (Cappella, 1991). The desire for synchronous patterns of behavior in personal relationships seems to carry on throughout people's lives. This belief is supported by Cappella's (1991) findings that "broad patterns of adult and infant-adult interactions are parallel to one another" (p. 18).

Control

Synchronous behaviors during dyadic interactions signal to the interactants that each partner is attending to the other and are an indication of a general state of rapport (Gatewood & Rosenwein, 1981). This state of rapport indicates to the interactants that they are in control of their relationship. Cappella (1984) found that individuals altered their talk and silence sequences as they switched to new partners. This suggests that quality communication is contingent on dyadic rhythm and behavioral synchrony.

This control also extends to some of the more static features of relational contact. For example, rooms can be arranged to promote or prohibit closer interactions because of the opportunity for extended eye gaze, close proximity, or even touch between the interactants (Burgoon et al., 1989). As with most issues of control, greater regulation of the situation leads to greater predictability of the interactions.

Mixed Messages and Deception

As noted by Mehrabian and Ferris (1967), a discrepancy between verbal and nonverbal channels creates a mixed message, with the end result being reliance on the nonverbal channels. Yet nonverbal cues alone can send mixed signals resulting in incongruous messages (Burgoon et al., 1989). These mixed messages can be premeditated or inadvertent, or hurtful or kind acts of deception, or simply may be indicative of indecision or confusion within personal relationships. This function is not addressed by Patterson's classification, yet it encompasses a very important area in personal relationships. Mixed messages may lead to uncertainty about the relationship or partner and very often are communicated with nonverbal cues. Deception in personal relationships often is seen as detrimental to personal relationships and is detected through leakage by nonverbal cues.

Positivity

The issue of whether mixed messages are positive or negative in dyadic relationships depends in large part on the reason for the ambiguous nonverbal cues. The positivity of a message is largely a function of how it is interpreted. For example, playful teasing (a form of mixed message) when viewed positively by the interactants can sometimes end a negative conflict spiral. However, when that same behavior is viewed as an inconsistent message, it is likely to increase the conflict (Alberts, 1990). Mixed messages contain both positive and negative cues but form a single message, whereas inconsistent cues, which often are construed as mixed messages, involve the masking of negative messages. Inconsistent messages are difficult to decode, frustrating for the interactants, and viewed negatively. In addition, inconsistent messages create suspicion between interactants and often are decoded as deception (Zuckerman, Driver, & Koestner, 1982).

Intimacy

Mixed messages and deception often are seen as being detrimental toward the ideal of intimacy. Encoders often experience negative reactions such as guilt and anxiety about being discovered (Ekman & Friesen, 1969). This may create some emotional distance between liars and their partners, which will have a negative impact on intimacy within the relationship. Liars usually "leak" nonverbal cues that include nervous and arousal cues, negative affect cues, and incompetent communication patterns (Buller & Burgoon, in press). These cues (e.g., eye blinking, increased self-touching, more speech hesitations) may send messages of distraction and reticence, which would be detrimental to the intimacy process.

Control

Deception is a method for controlling information (Burgoon et al., 1989). The motivation for deception in personal relationships is often to save face; to promote, maintain, or terminate a relationship; to establish or maintain power over a partner; to avoid conflict; or to maintain or end social interactions (Burgoon et al., 1989). In instances in which the "liars'" motivations are high (e.g., for the good of the partner or the relationship), and their arousal levels concerning the deception are low, detection of deception through nonverbal cue leakage will be reduced (Buller & Aune, 1987). If the deception is not discovered, then the person has successfully maintained some control of the relationship.

Social Influence

Nonverbal behaviors may be coordinated by individuals to intentionally influence their partners' perceptions, behaviors, or attitudes (Burgoon et al., 1989; Patterson, 1992). Individuals may purposely attempt to influence their partners by using specific nonverbal patterns of behavior (e.g., smiles versus frowns, encouraging touches versus a spanking, head nods versus head shakes, etc.).

Positivity

Positive and negative nonverbal feedback often influence quality communication in personal relationships. Positive feedback may include such nonverbal cues as smiling, nods, forward lean, frequent eye gaze, touching, and approving vocal cues (Burgoon et al., 1989). Positive nonverbal feedback cues have been found to increase the amount of feeling and self-reference statements made during dyadic interactions (Hackney, 1974). Thus positive feedback cues may increase the potential for the amount of relational talk, the judgment of positive interaction outcomes, and the value of the dyadic interaction. Conversely, negative feedback cues (e.g., reduced eye contact, frowns, scowls, knitted brows, neutral or negative facial expressions, silence, and cold or angry vocal cues) (Burgoon et al., 1989) may have a negative impact on personal relationships if they are seen to be punishing to either person in the interaction. Negative feedback cues

function to augment behaviors if they increase a desired behavior and to reprove if they extinguish or decrease disliked
behaviors. Quality communication between parents and their
children, as well as between romantic partners, often is affected
by the choice to use positive or negative feedback during dyadic
interactions.

Intimacy

Using nonverbal messages to foster a more intimate relationship is a major strategy for achieving social influence. Nonverbal
cues that signal greater connection and immediacy (e.g., increased
gaze, touch and gesturing, direct body and face orientation, increased facial expressiveness and pleasantness) have the ability
to change a partner's behaviors and attitudes during dyadic
interactions (Burgoon et al., 1989). Exercising social influence
through the use of these intimacy tactics should enhance the
quality of communication in personal relationships. However,
this may involve some risk. If the social influence obtained
through intimacy ultimately hurts the relationship or the person
who was persuaded, then the repercussions could have serious
negative consequences on the quality of communication for the
couple.

Control

The desire to affect future events in the relationship is associated with the function of exercising social control. In general,
relational patterns of reciprocity and compensation of exercising social control may be indicative of interactants' endeavor
for relational control. Ickes, Patterson, Rajecki, and Tanford
(1982) found that interactants who expected their partner to
be unpleasant encoded a compensatory pattern of nonverbal
involvement (e.g., greater facial pleasantness, more direct body
orientation, greater eye gaze, increased talking time) in an effort
to sway the partner's attitude and behavior.

Message Production,
Processing, and Comprehension

Patterson's final functional category highlights the importance of nonverbal cues for completing tasks. The general concept of completing tasks is mirrored by Burgoon et al.'s (1989) classification of message production, processing, and comprehension. This classification encompasses a broad array of tasks such as the central processing of information or learning of any new skills or concepts that are aided by the use of nonverbal behaviors (Burgoon et al., 1989).

Positivity

The ability to understand each other is fundamental to the communication process. If nonverbal cues are not effective in the production, processing, and comprehension of messages, then interactions are perceived negatively and quality communication is impaired. If, on the other hand, nonverbal cues effectively frame verbal utterances, focus and increase attention on verbal messages, enhance comprehension, and/or facilitate people's memory of interactions, then quality communication will be enhanced and dyadic exchanges will be perceived positively.

Intimacy

The link between intimacy and the nonverbal function of message production, processing, and comprehension is not an obvious one. Yet the role of nonverbal behaviors with respect to this function clearly is related to interactants' memory of events. Recall that intimacy is achieved through numerous exchanges, but relationships do not develop from nonstop, continuous exchanges. In reality, relationships "extend across numerous interactions and over a considerable period of time" (Sigman, 1991, p. 106). Thus memories of previous interactions play an important role in the development of intimate relationships. Nonverbal cues are critical for information processing, and therefore are partially responsible for what interactants remember about dyadic exchanges. Nonverbal behaviors often are remembered more accurately than verbal messages (Burgoon et al., 1989). So the consequential link between the ideal of intimacy and this last function lies with the impact of memory on the development of personal relationships over time.

Control

The ideal of control and facilitating service task goals, as well as message production, processing, and comprehension, are coordinated because interactive nonverbal patterns during service encounters often follow predictable and scripted routines (Patterson, 1992). The scripted routines allow for the predictability in dyadic interactions that is necessary for the perception of control within the relationship. Behaviors could not be synchronized or coordinated by partners without these scripted routines.

Conclusion

Quality communication is essential to personal relationships. Nonverbal behaviors are indicative of quality communication. Research indicates that people pay close attention to nonverbal behaviors as indicators of the health of their relationships. Ultimately, the health or illness of a relationship is judged by a couple's communication patterns. This research review illustrates the power and impact of nonverbal behaviors, not only on the communication patterns within dyadic interactions but also on the relationships themselves. Personal relationships are volatile and susceptible to a wide range of illnesses; consequently, nonverbal behaviors are monitored closely, especially during times of relational change. Individuals scrutinize and evaluate their own relationships in terms of quality communication, whether or not they actually are aware of it. The quality of communication as we know and experience it could not be determined without examination of nonverbal behaviors.

This chapter only hints at the wealth of knowledge that remains largely unexplored by scholars. Patterson's (1992) and Burgoon and associates' (1989) functional approaches to nonverbal behaviors offer a good starting point for the study of nonverbal symbols' impact on how we judge our relationships. The complexity and interdependence of nonverbal behaviors demand a holistic evaluation of their impact on quality communication. Only through this kind of holistic approach can nonverbal behavior's impact on quality communication be understood.

References

Acitelli, L. K. (1993). Awareness of self, partner, and relationship. In S. W. Duck (Ed.), *Understanding relationship processes: Vol. 1. Individuals and relationships* (pp. 144-174). Newbury Park, CA: Sage.

Acitelli, L. K., Douvan, E., & Veroff, J. (1993). Perceptions of conflict in the first year of marriage: How important are similarity and understanding? *Journal of Social and Personal Relationships, 10*, 5-19.

Acitelli, L. K., & Duck, S. W. (1987). Intimacy as the proverbial elephant. In D. Perlman & S. W. Duck (Eds.), *Intimate relationships: Development, dynamics and deterioration* (pp. 297-308). Newbury Park, CA: Sage.

Ainsworth, M. D. S., Blehar, M. C., Waters, E., & Wall, S. (1978). *Patterns of attachment: A psychological study of the strange situation.* Hillsdale, NJ: Lawrence Erlbaum.

Alberts, K. J. (1990). The use of humor in managing couples conflict interactions. In D. D. Cahn (Ed.), *Intimates in conflict: A communication perspective* (pp. 105-120). Hillsdale, NJ: Lea.

Altman, I. (1973). Reciprocity of interpersonal exchange. *Journal for the Theory of Social Behavior, 3*, 249-261.

Altman, I. (1993). Dialectics, physical environments, and personal relationships. *Communication Monographs, 60*, 26-34.

Altman, I., & Taylor, D. A. (1973). *Social penetration: The development of interpersonal relationships.* New York: Holt, Rinehart & Winston.

Altman, I., Vinsel, A., & Brown, B. H. (1981). Dialectic conceptions in social psychology: An application to social penetration and privacy regulation. In L. Berkowitz (Ed.), *Advances in experimental social psychology* (Vol. 14, pp. 107-160). New York: Academic Press.

Andersen, P. (1993). Cognition and processing of information in relationships. In S. W. Duck (Ed.), *Understanding relationship processes: Vol. 1. Individuals and relationships* (pp. 1-29). Newbury Park, CA: Sage.

Anderson, J., & Reder, L. (1979). Elaborative processing explanation of depth of processing. In L. S. Cermak & F. I. Craik (Eds.), *Levels of processing in human memory* (pp. 385-403). Hillsdale, NJ: Lawrence Erlbaum.

Archer, R. L. (1979). Anatomical and psychological sex differences. In G. J. Chelune, R. L. Archer, C. L. Kleinke, J. M. Civikly, V. J. Derlega, J. A. Doster, J. Grzelak, J. R. Herron, J. G. Nesbitt, L. B. Rosenfeld, D. A. Taylor, & J. Waterman (Eds.), *Self-disclosure: Origins, patterns, and implications of openness in interpersonal relationships* (pp. 80-109). San Francisco: Jossey-Bass.

Archer, R. L. (1987). Commentary: Self-disclosure, a very useful behavior. In V. J. Derlega & J. H. Berg (Eds.), *Self-disclosure: Theory, research, and therapy* (pp. 329-342). New York: Plenum.

Aristotle. (1932). *The rhetoric* (L. Cooper, Trans.). New York: Appleton-Century-Crofts. (Original work published c. 330 B.C.E.)

Aronson, E., & Worchel, S. (1966). Similarity versus liking as determinants of interpersonal attractiveness. *Psychonomic Science, 5,* 157-158.

Aukett, R., Ritchie, J., & Mill, K. (1988). Gender differences in friendship patterns. *Sex Roles, 19,* 57-66.

Baier, A. (1986). Trust and antitrust. *Ethics, 96,* 231-260.

Bartholomew, K. (1993). Attachment theory and relationships with others. In S. W. Duck (Ed.), *Understanding relationship processes: Vol. 2. Learning about relationships* (pp. 30-62). Newbury Park, CA: Sage.

Bavelas, J. B., Black, A., Chovil, N., & Mullet, J. (1990). *Equivocal communication.* Newbury Park, CA: Sage.

Baxter, L. A. (1987). Self-disclosure and relationship disengagement. In V. J. Derlega & J. H. Berg (Eds.), *Self-disclosure: Theory, research, and therapy* (pp. 155-174). New York: Plenum.

Baxter, L. A. (1988). A dialectical perspective on communication strategies in relationship development. In S. W. Duck (Ed.), *A handbook of personal relationships* (pp. 257-273). Chichester, UK: John Wiley.

Baxter, L. A. (1990). Dialectical contradictions in relationship development. *Journal of Social and Personal Relationships, 7,* 69-88.

Baxter, L. A. (1992). Root metaphors in accounts of developing romantic relationships. *Journal of Social and Personal Relationships, 9,* 253-275.

Baxter, L. A., & Wilmot, W. W. (1985). Taboo topics in close relationships. *Journal of Social and Personal Relationships, 2,* 253-269.

Beinstein Miller, J. (1993). Learning from early relationship experiences. In S. W. Duck (Ed.), *Understanding relationship processes: Vol. 2. Learning about relationships* (pp. 1-29). Newbury Park, CA: Sage.

Bell, R. A., & Healey, J. G. (1992). Idiomatic communication and interpersonal solidarity in friends' relational cultures. *Human Communication Research, 18,* 307-335.

Bennett, J. (in press). *Time: A process approach to relationships.* New York: Guilford.

Berg, J. H. (1987). Responsiveness and self-disclosure. In V. J. Derlega & J. H. Berg (Eds.), *Self-disclosure: Theory, research, and therapy.* New York: Plenum.

Berg, J. H., & Archer, R. L. (1980). Disclosure or concern: A second look at liking for the norm-breaker. *Journal of Personality, 48,* 245-257.

Berg, J. H., & Derlega, V. J. (1987). Themes in the study of self-disclosure. In V. J. Derlega & J. H. Berg (Eds.), *Self-disclosure: Theory, research, and therapy* (pp. 1-8). New York: Plenum.

Berger, C. R. (1993). Plans and strategies in relationships. In S. W. Duck (Ed.), *Understanding relationship processes: Vol. 1. Individuals and relationships* (pp. 30-59). Newbury Park, CA: Sage.

Berger, C. R., & Calabrese, R. J. (1975). Some explorations in initial interaction and beyond: Toward a developmental theory of interpersonal communication. *Human Communication Research, 1,* 99-112.

Berger, C. R., & Kellermann, K. A. (1983). To ask or not to ask: Is that a question? In R. Bostrom (Ed.), *Communication yearbook 7* (pp. 342-368). Newbury Park, CA: Sage.

Berscheid, E. (1983). Emotion. In H. H. Kelley, E. Berscheid, A. Christensen, J. H. Harvey, T. L. Huston, G. Levinger, E. McClintock, L. A. Peplau, & D. R. Peterson (Eds.), *Close relationships* (pp. 110-168). New York: W. H. Freeman.

Berscheid, E., & Walster [Hatfield], E. (1978). *Interpersonal attraction* (2nd ed.). Reading, MA: Addison-Wesley.

Billig, M. (1987). *Arguing and thinking: A rhetorical approach to social psychology.* Cambridge, UK: Cambridge University Press.

Bochner, A. P. (1982). On the efficacy of openness in closed relationships. In M. Burgoon (Ed.), *Communication yearbook 5* (pp. 109-124). New Brunswick, NJ: Transaction Books.

Bochner, A. P. (1991). On the paradigm that would not die. *Communication yearbook 14* (pp. 484-491).

Bok, S. (1983). *Secrets: On the ethics of concealment and revelation.* New York: Pantheon.

Boon, S. D. (1992). *Love hurts: An exploration of the psychology of risk in dating relationships.* Unpublished doctoral dissertation, University of Waterloo, Waterloo.

Boon, S. D., & Holmes, J. G. (1990, June). Insecurity in marriage: Relating research on interpersonal trust, attachment and emotion. In S. Desmarais (Chair), *Perspectives on the psychology of intimate relations: Research, theory and strategies.* Symposium conducted at the annual conference of the Canadian Psychological Association in Ottawa, Ontario, Canada.

Boon, S. D., & Holmes, J. G. (1991). The dynamics of interpersonal trust: Resolving uncertainty in the face of risk. In R. A. Hinde & J. Groebel (Eds.), *Cooperation and prosocial behaviour* (pp. 190-211). Cambridge, UK: Cambridge University Press.

Bowlby, J. (1973). *Attachment and loss: Vol. 2. Separation: Anxiety and anger.* New York: Basic Books.

Braiker, H. G., & Kelley, H. H. (1979). Conflict in the development of close relationships. In R. L. Burgess & T. L. Huston (Eds.), *Social exchange in developing relationships* (pp. 135-168). New York: Academic Press.

Bretherton, I. (1990). Communication patterns, internal working models, and the intergenerational transmission of attachment relationships. *Infant Mental Health Journal, 11,* 237-252.

Brickman, P. (1987). *Commitment, conflict and caring.* Englewood Cliffs, NJ: Prentice Hall.

Brown, P., & Levinson, S. (1987). *Politeness: Some universals in language use.* Cambridge, UK: Cambridge University Press.

Buller, D. B., & Aune, R. K. (1987). Nonverbal cues to deception among intimates, friends, and strangers. *Journal of Nonverbal Behavior, 11,* 269-290.

Buller, D. B., & Burgoon, J. K. (in press). Deception. In J. A. Daly & J. M. Wiemann (Eds.), *Communicating strategically: Strategies in interpersonal communication.* Hillsdale, NJ: Lawrence Erlbaum.

Burgoon, J. K. (1980). Nonverbal communication research in the 1970s. In D. Nimmo (Ed.), *Communication yearbook 4* (pp. 179-197). New Brunswick, NJ: Transaction Books.

Burgoon, J. K. (1982). Privacy in communication. In M. Burgoon (Ed.), *Communication yearbook 6* (pp. 206-249). Newbury Park, CA: Sage.

Burgoon, J. K. (1985). Nonverbal signals. In M. L. Knapp & G. R. Miller (Eds.), *Handbook of interpersonal communication* (pp. 344-390). Beverly Hills, CA: Sage.

Burgoon, J. K., Buller, D. B., Hale, J. L., & deTurck, M. A. (1984). Relational messages associated with nonverbal behaviors. *Human Communication Research, 10,* 351-378.

Burgoon, J. K., Buller, D. B., & Woodall, W. G. (1989). *Nonverbal communication: The unspoken dialogue.* New York: Harper & Row.

Burgoon, J. K., & Hale, J. L. (1984). The fundamental topoi of relational communication. *Communication Monographs, 51,* 193-214.

Burleson, B., & Denton, W. (1992). A new look at similarity and attraction in marriage: Similarities in social-cognitive and communication skills as predictors of attraction and satisfaction. *Communication Monographs, 59,* 268-287.

Byers, P., & Byers, H. (1972). Nonverbal communication and the education of children. In C. B. Cazden, V. P. John, & D. Hymes (Eds.), *Functions of language in the classroom* (pp. 3-31). New York: Teachers College Press.

Byrne, D. (1961). Interpersonal attraction and attitude similarity. *Journal of Abnormal and Social Psychology, 62,* 713-715.

Byrne, D. (1971). *The attraction paradigm.* New York: Academic Press.

Byrne, D. (1992). The transition from controlled laboratory experimentation to less controlled settings: Surprise! Additional variables are operative. *Communication Monographs, 59,* 190-198.

Byrne, D., Ervin, C. R., & Lamberth, J. (1970). Continuity between the experimental study of attraction and real-life computer dating. *Journal of Personality and Social Psychology, 16,* 157-165.

Byrne, D., & Griffitt, W. (1966). Similarity versus liking: A clarification. *Psychonomic Science, 6,* 295-296.

Byrne, D., & Lamberth, J. (1971). Cognitive and reinforcement theories as complementary approaches to the study of attraction. In B. I. Murstein (Ed.), *Theories of attraction and love* (pp. 59-84). New York: Springer.

Campbell, D. T. (1963). Social attitudes and other acquired behavioral dispositions. In D. Koch (Ed.), *Psychology: A study of a science* (pp. 94-172). New York: McGraw-Hill.

Cappella, J. N. (1984). The relevance of the microstructure of interaction to relationship change. *Journal of Social and Personal Relationships, 1,* 239-264.

Cappella, J. N. (1991). The biological origins of automated patterns of human interaction. *Communication Theory, 1,* 4-35.

Cappella, J. N., & Palmer, M. (1990). Attitude similarity, relational history, and attraction: The mediating effects of kinesic and vocal behavior. *Communication Monographs, 57,* 161-183.

Cappella, J. N., & Palmer, M. (1992). The effect of partners' conversation on the association between attitude similarity and attraction. *Communication Monographs, 59,* 180-189.

Chelune, G. J. (1979). Measuring openness in interpersonal communication. In G. J. Chelune & associates (Eds.), *Self-disclosure: Origins, patterns, and implications of openness in interpersonal relationships* (pp. 1-27). San Francisco: Jossey-Bass.

Chi, M. T. H., Glaser, R., & Farr, M. J. (1988). *The nature of expertise.* Hillsdale, NJ: Lawrence Erlbaum.

Chiesi, H. L., Spilich, G. J., & Voss, J. F. (1979). Acquisition of domain-related information in relation to high and low domain knowledge. *Journal of Verbal Learning and Verbal Behavior, 18,* 257-273.

Cissna, K., & Sieburg, E. (1981). Patterns of interactional confirmation and disconfirmation. In C. Wilder-Mott & J. Weakland (Eds.), *Rigor and imagination: Essays from the legacy of Gregory Bateson.* New York: Praeger.

Clark, H. H. (1992). *Arenas of language use.* Chicago: University of Chicago Press.

Clark, H. H., & Haviland, S. E. (1977). Comprehension and the given-new contract. In R. O. Freedle (Ed.), *Discourse production and comprehension* (pp. 1-40). Norwood, NJ: Ablex.

Clark, H. H., & Marshall, C. R. (1981). Definite reference and mutual knowledge. In A. K. Joshi, B. L. Webber, & I. A. Sag (Eds.), *Elements of discourse understanding* (pp. 10-63). Cambridge, UK: Cambridge University Press.

Clark, H. H., & Schaefer, E. F. (1987). Concealing one's meaning from overhearers. *Journal of Memory and Language, 26,* 209-225.

Clark, H. H., & Schaefer, E. F. (1989). Contributing to discourse. *Cognitive Science, 13,* 259-294.

Cline, R. J. (1982, May). *Revealing and relating: A review of self-disclosure theory and research.* Paper presented at the International Communication Association Convention, Boston.

Cline, R. J. (1983, November). *Promising new directions for teaching and research: Self-disclosure.* Paper presented at the annual convention of the Speech Communication Association, Washington, DC.

Collins, N. L., & Miller, L. C. (1993). *The disclosure-liking link: From meta-analysis towards a dynamic reconceptualization.* Unpublished manuscript, State University of New York at Buffalo.

Collins, N. L., & Read, S. J. (1990). Adult attachment, working models, and relationship quality in dating couples. *Journal of Personality and Social Psychology, 58,* 644-663.

Condon, W. S., & Sander, L. W. (1974). Synchrony demonstrated between movement of the neonate and adult speech. *Child Development, 45,* 456-462.

Coupland, J., Coupland, N., Giles, H., & Wiemann, J. (1988). My life is in your hands: Processes of self-disclosure in intergenerational talk. In N. Coupland (Ed.), *Styles of discourse.* London: Croom Helm.

Cozby, P. C. (1973). Self-disclosure: A literature review. *Psychological Bulletin, 79,* 73-91.

Davis, M. S. (1973). *Intimate relations.* New York: Free Press.

Dawes, R. M. (1988). *Rational choice in an uncertain world.* Toronto, Ontario: Harcourt Brace Jovanovich.

Derlega, V. J., Metts, S., Petronio, S., & Margulis, S. T. (1993). *Self-disclosure.* Newbury Park, CA: Sage.

Derlega, V. J., Wilson, J., & Chaikin, A. L. (1976). Friendship and disclosure reciprocity. *Journal of Personality and Social Psychology, 34,* 578-582.

Deutsch, M. (1958). Trust and suspicion. *Journal of Conflict Resolution, 2,* 265-279.

DeVito, J. A., & Hecht, M. L. (1990). *The nonverbal communication reader.* Prospect Heights, IL: Waveland.

Dindia, K. (1982). Reciprocity of self-disclosure: A sequential analysis. In M. Burgoon (Ed.), *Communication yearbook 6* (pp. 506-528). Newbury Park, CA: Sage.

Dindia, K. (1984, May). *Antecedents and consequents of self-disclosure.* Paper presented at the meeting of the International Communication Association, San Francisco.

Dindia, K. (1988). A comparison of several statistical tests of reciprocity of self-disclosure. *Communication Research, 15,* 726-752.

Dindia, K., & Allen, M. (1992). Sex-differences in self-disclosure: A meta-analysis. *Psychological Bulletin, 112,* 106-124.

Dindia, K., Fitzpatrick, M. A., & Kenny, D. A. (1989, May). *Self-disclosure in spouse and stranger dyads: A social relations analysis.* Paper presented at the meeting of the International Communication Association, San Francisco.

Dixson, M., & Duck, S. W. (1992). Understanding relationship processes: Uncovering the human search for meaning. In S. W. Duck (Ed.), *Understanding relationship processes: Vol. 1. Individuals in relationships* (pp. 175-206). Newbury Park, CA: Sage.

Dosser, D., Balswick, J., & Halverson, C. (1986). Male inexpressiveness and relationships. *Journal of Social and Personal Relationships, 3,* 241-256.

Douglas, W. (1984). Initial interaction scripts: When knowing is behaving. *Human Communication Research, 11,* 203-219.

Duck, S. W. (1976). Interpersonal communication in developing acquaintance. In G. Miller (Ed.), *Explorations in interpersonal communication* (pp. 127-147). Beverly Hills, CA: Sage.

Duck, S. W. (1980). Personal relationships research in the 1980s: Towards an understanding of complex human sociality. *Western Journal of Speech Communication, 44,* 114-119.

Duck, S. W. (1982). A topography of relationship disengagement and dissolution. In S. W. Duck (Ed.), *Personal relationships 4: Dissolving personal relationships.* London: Academic Press.

Duck, S. W. (1988). *Relating to others.* Monterey, CA: Dorsey, Brooks & Cole.

Duck, S. W. (1990). Relationships as unfinished business: Out of the frying pan and into the 1990s. *Journal of Social and Personal Relationships, 7,* 5-29.

Duck, S. W. (1994a). *Meaningful relationships: Talking, sense, and relating.* Thousand Oaks, CA: Sage.

Duck, S. W. (1994b). Stratagems, spoils, and a serpent's tooth: On the delights and dilemmas of personal relationships. In W. R. Cupach & B. H. Spitzberg (Eds.), *The dark side of interpersonal communication* (pp. 3-24). Hillsdale, NJ: Lea.

Duck, S. W., & Barnes, M. K. (1992). Disagreeing about agreement: Reconciling differences about similarity. *Communication Monographs, 59,* 199-208.

Duck, S. W., & Craig, R. G. (1978). Personality similarity and the development of friendship: A longitudinal study. *British Journal of Social Clinical Psychology, 17,* 237-242.

Duck, S. W., & Miell, D. K. (1986). Charting the development of personal relationships. In R. Gilmour & S. W. Duck (Eds.), *The emerging field of personal relationships* (pp. 133-143). Hillsdale, NJ: Lawrence Erlbaum.

Duck, S. W., Rutt, D. J., Hurst, M. H., & Strejc, H. (1991). Some evident truths about conversations in everyday relationships: All communications are not created equal. *Human Communication Research, 18,* 228-267.

Eidelson, R. J. (1980). Interpersonal satisfaction and level of involvement: A curvilinear relationship. *Journal of Personality and Social Psychology, 39,* 460-470.

Ekman, P., & Friesen, W. V. (1969). Nonverbal leakage and clues to deception. *Psychiatry, 32,* 88-106.

Ekman, P., Friesen, W. V., & Ancoli, S. (1980). Facial signs of emotional experience. *Journal of Personality and Social Psychology, 39,* 1125-1134.

Ericsson, K. A., & Smith, J. (1991). Prospects and limits of the empirical study of expertise: An introduction. In K. A. Ericsson & J. Smith (Eds.), *Toward a general theory of expertise* (pp. 1-38). Cambridge, UK: Cambridge University Press.

Erikson, E. H. (1963). *Childhood and society* (rev. ed.). New York: Norton.

Erikson, E. H. (1968). *Identity, youth and crisis.* New York: Norton.

Fletcher, G. J. O., & Fitness, J. (1993). Knowledge structures and explanations in intimate relationships. In S. W. Duck (Ed.), *Understanding relationship processes: Vol. 1. Individuals and relationships* (pp. 121-143). Newbury Park, CA: Sage.

Furnham, A., & Argyle, M. (1981). *The psychology of social situations: Selected readings.* New York: Pergamon.

Gard, L. (1990). Patient disclosure of human immunodeficiency virus (HIV) status to parents: Clinical considerations. *Professional Psychology: Research and Practice, 21,* 252-256.

Gatewood, J. B., & Rosenwein, R. (1981). Interactional synchrony: Genuine or spurious? A critique of recent research. *Journal of Nonverbal Behavior, 6,* 12-29.

Gershman, H. (1983). The stress of coming out. *The American Journal of Psychoanalysis, 43,* 129-138.

Gibran, K. (1923). *The prophet.* New York: Knopf.

Gilbert, D. T. (1989). Thinking lightly about others: Automatic components of the social inference process. In J. S. Uleman & J. A. Bargh (Eds.), *Unintended thought* (pp. 189-211). New York: Guilford.

Gilbert, S. J., & Horenstein, D. (1975). The communication of self-disclosure: Level versus valence. *Human Communication Research, 1,* 316-322.

Glaser, R., & Chi, M. T. H. (1988). Overview. In M. T. H. Chi, R. Glaser, & M. J. Farr (Eds.), *The nature of expertise* (pp. xv-xxii). Hillsdale, NJ: Lawrence Erlbaum.

Goffman, E. (1963). *Stigma: Notes on the management of spoiled identity.* New York: Simon & Schuster.

Goldberg, J. A. (1983). A move toward describing conversational coherence. In R. T. Craig & K. Tracy (Eds.), *Conversational coherence* (pp. 25-45). Beverly Hills, CA: Sage.

Gottman, J. M. (1991). Predicting the longitudinal course of marriages. *Journal of Marital and Family Therapy, 17,* 3-7.

Gottman, J. M., & Krokoff, L. J. (1989). Marital interaction and satisfaction: A longitudinal view. *Journal of Consulting and Clinical Psychology, 57,* 47-52.

Gottman, J. M., Markman, H., & Notarius, C. (1977). The topography of marital conflict: A sequential analysis of verbal and nonverbal behavior. *Journal of Marriage and the Family, 39,* 461-477.

Gouldner, A. W. (1960). The norm of reciprocity: A preliminary statement. *American Sociological Review, 25,* 161-178.

Grice, H. P. (1975). Logic and conversation. In P. Cole & J. L. Morgan (Eds.), *Syntax and semantics 3: Speech acts* (pp. 41-58). New York: Academic Press.

Grotevant, H. D., & Cooper, C. R. (1985). Patterns of interaction in family relationships and the development of identity exploration in adolescence. *Child Development, 56,* 415-428.

Grotevant, H. D., & Cooper, C. R. (1986). Individuation in family relationships. *Human Development, 29,* 82-100.

Hackney, H. (1974). Facial gestures and subject expression of feelings. *Journal of Counseling Psychology, 21,* 173-178.

Hansson, R. O., Jones, W. H., & Fletcher, W. L. (1990). Troubled relationships in later life: Implications for support. *Journal of Social and Personal Relationships, 7,* 451-463.

Hauser, S. T., Book, B. K., Houlihan, J., Powers, S., Weiss-Perry, B., Follansbee, D., Jacobson, A. M., & Noam, G. G. (1987). Sex differences within the family: Studies of adolescent and parent family interaction. *Journal of Youth and Adolescence, 16,* 199-220.

Hauser, S. T., Powers, S. I., Noam, G. G., Jacobson, A. M., Weiss, B., & Follansbee, D. J. (1984). Familial contexts of adolescent ego development. *Child Development, 55,* 195-213.

Hazan, C., & Shaver, P. (1987). Romantic love conceptualized as an attachment process. *Journal of Personality and Social Psychology, 52,* 511-524.

Helgeson, V. S., Shaver, P., & Dyer, M. (1987). Prototypes of intimacy and distance in same-sex and opposite-sex relationships. *Journal of Social and Personal Relationships, 4,* 195-233.

Heritage, J. (1984). A change-of-state token and aspects of its sequential placement. In J. M. Atkinson & J. Heritage (Eds.), *Structures of social action: Studies in conversational analysis* (pp. 299-345). Cambridge, UK: Cambridge University Press.

Hewes, D., & Planalp, S. (1982). "There is nothing as useful as a good theory . . .": The influence of social knowledge on interpersonal communication. In M. Roloff & C. Berger (Eds.), *Social cognition and communication* (pp. 107-150). Beverly Hills, CA: Sage.

Hill, C. T., & Stull, D. E. (1982). Disclosure reciprocity: Conceptual and measurement issues. *Social Psychology Quarterly, 45,* 238-244.

Holmberg, D., & Holmes, J. G. (in press). Reconstruction of relationship memories: A mental models approach. In N. Schwartz & S. Sudman (Eds.), *Autobiographical memory and the validity of retrospective reports.* New York: Springer Verlag.

Holmes, J. G. (1991). Trust and the appraisal process in close relationships. In W. H. Jones & D. Perlman (Eds.), *Advances in personal relationships* (Vol. 2, pp. 57-104). London: Jessica Kingsley.

Holmes, J. G., & Rempel, J. K. (1989). Trust in close relationships. In C. Hendrick (Ed.), *Review of personality and social psychology: Vol. 10. Close relationships* (pp. 187-220). Newbury Park, CA: Sage.

Holtzworth-Munroe, A., & Jacobson, N. S. (1985). Causal attributions of married couples: When do they search for causes? What do they conclude when they do? *Journal of Personality and Social Psychology, 48,* 1398-1412.

Hurvitz, N. (1970). Interaction hypotheses in marriage counseling. *Family Coordinator, 19,* 64-75.

Ickes, W., Patterson, M. L., Rajecki, D. W., & Tanford, S. (1982). Behavioral and cognitive consequences of reciprocal versus compensatory responses to preinteraction expectancies. *Social Cognition, 1,* 160-190.

Ickes, W., Tooke, W., Stinson, L., Baker, V., & Bissonnette, V. (1988). Naturalistic social cognition: Intersubjectivity in same-sex dyads. *Journal of Nonverbal Behavior, 12,* 58-84.

Isaacs, E. A., & Clark, H. H. (1987). References in conversation between experts and novices. *Journal of Experimental Psychology: General, 116,* 26-37.

Janoff-Bulman, R. (1992). *Shattered assumptions.* New York: Free Press.

Jones, W. H., Hobbs, S. A., & Hockenbury, D. (1982). Loneliness and social skill deficits. *Journal of Personality and Social Psychology, 42,* 682-689.

Jourard, S. M. (1971). *The transparent self* (rev. ed.). New York: Van Nostrand Reinhold.

Jourard, S. M., & Lasakow, P. (1958). Some factors in self-disclosure. *Journal of Abnormal Psychology, 56,* 91-98.

Kalbfleisch, P. J. (Ed.). (1993). *Interpersonal communication: Evolving personal relationships.* Hillsdale, NJ: Lawrence Erlbaum.

Katovich, M. A., & Couch, C. J. (1992). The nature of social pasts and their use as foundations for situated action. *Symbolic Interaction, 15,* 25-47.

Katriel, T., & Philipsen, G. (1981). What we need is communication: Communication as a cultural category in some American speech. *Communication Monographs, 48,* 301-317.

Kelley, H. H. (1979). *Personal relationships: Their structure and process.* Hillsdale, NJ: Lawrence Erlbaum.

Kelley, H. H. (1983). Love and commitment. In H. H. Kelley, E. Berscheid, A. Christensen, J. H. Harvey, T. L. Huston, G. Levinger, E. McClintock, L. A. Peplau, & D. R. Peterson (Eds.), *Close relationships* (pp. 265-314). New York: Freeman.

Kelley, H. H., & Stahelski, A. J. (1970). Social interaction basis of cooperators' and competitors' beliefs about others. *Journal of Personality and Social Psychology, 16,* 66-91.

Kelley, H. H., & Thibaut, J. W. (1978). *Interpersonal relations: A theory of interdependence*. New York: John Wiley.

Kelly, C., Huston, T. L., & Cate, R. M. (1985). Premarital relationship correlates of the erosion of satisfaction in marriage. *Journal of Social and Personal Relationships, 2,* 167-178.

Kelly, G. A. (1969). Ontological acceleration. In B. Maher (Ed.), *Clinical psychology and personality: The collected papers of George Kelly* (pp. 7-45). New York: John Wiley.

Kelly, G. A. (1970). Behavior is an experiment. In D. Bannister (Ed.), *Perspectives in personal construct theory* (pp. 1-26). London: Academic Press.

Kelvin, P. (1977). Predictability, power and vulnerability in interpersonal attraction. In S. W. Duck (Ed.), *Theory and practice in interpersonal attraction* (pp. 354-378). London: Academic Press.

Kent, G. G., Davis, J. D., & Shapiro, D. A. (1981). Effect of mutual acquaintance on the construction of conversation. *Journal of Experimental Social Psychology, 17,* 197-209.

Kidd, V. (1975). Happily ever after and other relationship styles: Advice on interpersonal relations in popular magazines, 1951-1973. *Quarterly Journal of Speech, 61,* 31-39.

Klein, R., & Milardo, R. (1993). Third-party influences on the development and maintenance of personal relationships. In S. W. Duck (Ed.), *Understanding relationship processes: Vol. 3. Social context and relationships* (pp. 55-77). Newbury Park, CA: Sage.

Knapp, M. L. (1983). Dyadic relationship development. In J. M. Wiemann & R. P. Harrison (Eds.), *Nonverbal interaction* (pp. 179-207). Beverly Hills, CA: Sage.

Knapp, M. L., & Comadena, M. E. (1979). Telling it like it isn't: A review of theory and research on deceptive communications. *Human Communication Research, 5,* 270-285.

Kobak, R. R., & Hazan, C. (1991). Attachment in marriage: Effects of security and accuracy of working models. *Journal of Personality and Social Psychology, 60,* 861-869.

Kreckel, M. (1981). *Communicative acts and shared knowledge in natural discourse.* London: Academic Press.

Kruglanski, A. (1990). Motivations for judging and knowing: Implications for causal attribution. In R. M. Sorrentino & E. T. Higgins (Eds.), *Handbook of motivation and cognition: Vol. 2. Foundations of social behaviour* (pp. 333-368). New York: Guilford.

Kunda, Z. (1990). The case for motivated reasoning. *Psychological Bulletin, 108,* 480-498.

La Gaipa, J. J. (1987). Friendship expectations. In R. Burnett, P. McGhee, & D. Clarke (Eds.), *Accounting for relationships: Explanation, representation and knowledge* (pp. 134-157). New York: Methuen.

LaFollette, H., & Graham, G. (1986). Honesty and intimacy. *Journal of Social and Personal Relationships, 3,* 3-18.

Laing, R. D., Phillipson, H., & Lee, R. (1966). *Interpersonal perception.* Baltimore, MD: Perennial Library.

Lea, M., & Spears, R. (in press). Relationships conducted over electronic systems. In J. T. Wood & S. W. Duck (Eds.), *Understanding relationship processes: Vol. 6. Understudied relationships.* Thousand Oaks, CA: Sage.

Leary, M. L., Rogers, P. A., Canfield, R. W., & Coe, C. (1986). Boredom in interpersonal encounters: Antecedents and social implications. *Journal of Personality and Social Psychology, 51,* 968-975.

Levenson, R. W., & Gottman, J. M. (1983). Marital interaction: Physiological linkage and affective exchange. *Journal of Personality and Social Psychology, 45,* 587-597.

Levenson, R. W., & Gottman, J. M. (1985). Physiological and affective predictors of change in relationship satisfaction. *Journal of Personality and Social Psychology, 49,* 85-94.

Lewis, J. D., & Weigert, A. J. (1985a). Social atomism, holism and trust. *The Sociological Quarterly, 26,* 455-471.

Lewis, J. D., & Weigert, A. J. (1985b). Trust as social reality. *Social Forces, 63,* 967-985.

Limandri, B. (1989). Disclosure of stigmatizing conditions: The discloser's perspective. *Archives of Psychiatric Nursing, 3,* 69-78.

Luhmann, N. (1988). Familiarity, confidence, trust: Problems and alternatives. In D. Gambetta (Ed.), *Trust: Making and breaking cooperative relations* (pp. 94-107). New York: Basil Blackwell.

MacFarlane, I., & Krebs, S. (1986). Techniques for interviewing and evidence gathering. In K. MacFarlane & J. Waterman (Eds.), *Sexual abuse of young children* (pp. 67-100). New York: Guilford.

Main, M., Kaplan, N., & Cassidy, J. (1985). Security in infancy, childhood, and adulthood: A move to the level of representation. In I. Bretherton & E. Waters (Eds.), *Growing points in attachment theory and research. Monographs of the Society for Research in Child Development, 50,* 66-106.

Markel, N. N., Phillis, J. A., Vargas, R., & Howard, K. (1972). Personality traits associated with voice types. *Journal of Psycholinguistic Research, 1,* 249-255.

Marks, G., Bundek, N., Richardson, J., Ruiz, M., Maldonado, N., & Mason, J. (1992). Self-disclosure of HIV infection: Preliminary results from a sample of Hispanic men. *Health Psychology, 11,* 300-306.

Maynard, D. W., & Zimmerman, D. H. (1984). Topical talk, ritual and the social organization of relationships. *Social Psychology Quarterly, 47,* 301-316.

McAdams, D. P., Jackson, R. J., & Kirshnit, C. (1984). Looking, laughing, and smiling in dyads as a function of intimacy motivation and reciprocity. *Journal of Personality, 52,* 261-273.

McKinney, D. H., & Donaghy, W. C. (1993). Dyadic gender structure, uncertainty reduction, and self-disclosure during initial interaction. In P. J. Kalbfleisch (Ed.), *Interpersonal communication: Evolving personal relationships.* Hillsdale, NJ: Lawrence Erlbaum.

Means, M. L., & Voss, J. F. (1985). Star wars: A developmental study of expert and novice knowledge structures. *Journal of Memory and Language, 24,* 746-757.

Mehrabian, A. (1981). *Silent messages: Implicit communication of emotions and attitudes* (2nd ed.). Belmont, CA: Wadsworth.

Mehrabian, A., & Ferris, S. R. (1967). Inference of attitudes from nonverbal communication in two channels. *Journal of Consulting Psychology, 31,* 248-252.

Merton, R. K. (1948). The self-fulfilling prophecy. *Antioch Review, 8,* 193-210.

Miell, D. E. (1984). *Cognitive and communicative strategies in developing relationships.* Unpublished doctoral dissertation, University of Lancaster.

Miell, D. E., & Duck, S. W. (1986). Strategies in developing friendships. In V. J. Derlega & B. A. Winstead (Eds.), *Friendship and social interaction* (pp. 129-143). New York: Springer Verlag.

Miller, D. T., & Turnbull, W. (1986). Expectancies and interpersonal processes. *Annual Review of Psychology, 37,* 233-256.

Miller, G. R., & Parks, M. R. (1982). Communication in dissolving relationships. In S. W. Duck (Ed.), *Personal relationships 4: Dissolving personal relationships* (pp. 127-154). London: Academic Press.

Miller, L. C. (1990). Intimacy and liking: Mutual influence and the role of unique relationships. *Journal of Personality and Social Psychology, 59,* 50-60.

Miller, L. C., & Kenny, D. A. (1986). Reciprocity of self-disclosure at the individual and dyadic levels: A social relations analysis. *Journal of Personality and Social Psychology, 50,* 713-719.

Monsour, M., Betty, S., & Kurzweil, N. (1993). Levels of perspectives and the perception of intimacy in cross-sex friendships: A balance theory explanation of shared perceptual reality. *Journal of Social and Personal Relationships, 10,* 529-550.

Montgomery, B. M. (1988). Quality communication in personal relationships. In S. W. Duck (Ed.), *Handbook of personal relationships* (pp. 343-366). New York: John Wiley.

Montgomery, B. M. (1993). Relationship maintenance versus relationship change: A dialectical dilemma. *Journal of Social and Personal Relationships, 10,* 205-224.

Morris, D. (1977). *Manwatching: A field guide to human behavior.* New York: Abrams.

Morton, T. L. (1978). Intimacy and reciprocity of exchange: A comparison of spouses and strangers. *Journal of Personality and Social Psychology, 36,* 72-81.

Murstein, B., & MacDonald, M. G. (1983). The relationship of the "exchange-orientation" and "commitment" scales to marriage adjustment. *International Journal of Psychology, 18,* 297-311.

Neuberg, S., Judice, N., Virdin, L., & Carrillo, M. (1993). Perceiver self-presentational goals as moderators of expectancy influences: Ingratiation and the disconfirmation of negative expectancies. *Journal of Personality and Social Psychology, 64,* 409-420.

Newcomb, T. M. (1956). The prediction of interpersonal attraction. *American Psychologist, 11,* 575-586.

Nofsinger, R. E. (1989). Collaborating on context: Invoking alluded-to shared knowledge. *Western Journal of Speech Communication, 53,* 227-241.

Noller, P. (1984). *Nonverbal communication and marital interaction.* Oxford, UK: Pergamon.

Noller, P., & Venardos, C. (1986). Communication awareness in married couples. *Journal of Social and Personal Relationships, 3,* 31-42.

Parks, M. (1982). Ideology in interpersonal communication: Off the couch and into the world. In M. Burgoon (Ed.), *Communication yearbook 5* (pp. 79-108). New Brunswick, NJ: Transaction Books.

Patterson, M. L. (1982). A sequential function model of nonverbal exchange. *Psychological Review, 89,* 231-249.

Patterson, M. L. (1983). *Nonverbal behavior: A functional perspective.* New York: Springer Verlag.

Patterson, M. L. (1987). Presentational and affect-management functions of nonverbal involvement. *Journal of Nonverbal Behavior, 11,* 110-122.

Patterson, M. L. (1992). A functional approach to nonverbal exchange. In R. S. Feldman & B. Rime (Eds.), *Fundamentals of nonverbal behavior* (pp. 458-495). New York: Cambridge University Press.

Pearce, W. B., & Sharp, S. M. (1973). Self-disclosing communication. *Journal of Communication, 23,* 409-425.

Perlman, D., & Fehr, B. (1987). The development of intimate relationships. In D. Perlman & S. W. Duck (Eds.), *Intimate relationships: Development, dynamics, and deterioration* (pp. 13-41). Beverly Hills, CA: Sage.

Petronio, S. (1988, November). *The dissemination of private information: The use of a boundary control system as an alternative perspective to the study of disclosures.* Paper presented at the Speech Communication Association Convention, New Orleans, LA.

Petronio, S. (1991). Communication boundary management: A theoretical model of managing disclosure of private information between marital couples. *Communication Theory, 1,* 311-335.

Pike, G. R., & Sillars, A. L. (1985). Reciprocity of marital communication. *Journal of Social and Personal Relationships, 2,* 303-324.

Planalp, S. (1985). Relational schemata: A test of alternative forms of relational knowledge as guides to communication. *Human Communication Research, 12,* 1-29.

Planalp, S. (1993). Friends' and acquaintances' conversations II: Coded differences. *Journal of Social and Personal Relationships, 10,* 339-354.

Planalp, S., & Benson, A. (1992). Friends' and acquaintances' conversations I: Observed differences. *Journal of Social and Personal Relationships, 9,* 483-506.

Planalp, S., & Honeycutt, J. M. (1985). Events that increase uncertainty in personal relationships. *Human Communication Research, 11,* 593-604.

Prusank, D. T., Duran, R. L., & DeLillo, D. A. (1993). Interpersonal relationships in women's magazines: Dating and relating in the 1970s and 1980s. *Journal of Social and Personal Relationships, 10,* 307-320.

Quintana, S. M., & Kerr, J. (1993). Relational needs in late adolescent separation-individuation. *Journal of Counseling and Development, 71,* 349-354.

Rawlins, W. K. (1983). Openness as problematic in ongoing friendships: Two conversational dilemmas. *Communication Monographs, 50,* 1-13.

Rawlins, W. K., & Holl, M. R. (1988). Adolescents' interaction with parents and friends: Dialectics of temporal perspective and evaluation. *Journal of Social and Personal Relationships, 5,* 27-46.

Register, L. M., & Henley, T. B. (1992). The phenomenology of intimacy. *Journal of Social and Personal Relationships, 9,* 467-481.

Reis, H. T., Senchak, M., & Soloman, B. (1985). Sex differences in the intimacy of social interaction: Further examination of potential explanations. *Journal of Personality and Social Psychology, 48,* 1204-1217.

Reis, H. T., & Shaver, P. (1988). Intimacy as an interpersonal process. In S. W. Duck (Ed.), *Handbook of personal relationships* (pp. 367-389). Chichester, UK: John Wiley.

Rempel, J. K., Holmes, J. G., & Zanna, M. P. (1985). Trust in close relationships. *Journal of Personality and Social Psychology, 49,* 95-112.

Reno, R. R., & Kenny, D. A. (1992). Effects of self-consciousness and social anxiety on self-disclosure among unacquainted individuals: An application of the social relations model. *Journal of Personality, 60,* 79-94.

Rodin, M. J. (1982). Non-engagement, failure to engage, and disengagement. In S. W. Duck (Ed.), *Personal relationships 4: Dissolving personal relationships* (pp. 31-49). New York: Academic Press.

Rohlfing, M. (in press). Long-distance and commuter partnerships. In J. T. Wood & S. W. Duck (Eds.), *Understanding relationship processes: Vol. 6. Understudied relationships.* Thousand Oaks, CA: Sage.

Rokeach, M. (1972). *Beliefs, attitudes, and values: A theory of organization and change.* San Francisco: Jossey-Bass.

Rosenbaum, M. E. (1986). The repulsion hypothesis: On the nondevelopment of relationships. *Journal of Personality and Social Psychology, 51,* 1156-1166.

Ross, L., & Nisbett, R. E. (1991). *The person and the situation: Perspectives of social psychology.* Toronto, Ontario: McGraw-Hill.

Rubin, Z. (1974). Lovers and other strangers: The development of intimacy in encounters and relationships. *American Scientist, 62,* 182-190.

Rusbult, C. E. (1983). A longitudinal test of the investment model: The development (and deterioration) of satisfaction and commitment in heterosexual involvement. *Journal of Personality and Social Psychology, 45,* 101-117.

Ryan, R. M., & Lynch, J. H. (1989). Emotional autonomy versus detachment: Revisiting the vicissitudes of adolescence and young adulthood. *Child Development, 60,* 340-356.

Sabatelli, R. M., Buck, R., & Kenny, D. A. (1986). A social relations analysis of nonverbal communication accuracy in married couples. *Journal of Personality, 54,* 513-527.

Scardamalia, M., & Bereiter, C. (1991). Literate expertise. In K. A. Ericsson & J. Smith (Eds.), *Toward a general theory of expertise* (pp. 172-194). Cambridge, UK: Cambridge University Press.

Schegloff, E. A. (1992). Repair after next turn: The last structurally provided defense of intersubjectivity in conversation. *American Journal of Sociology, 97,* 1295-1345.

Schutz, A. (1967). *The phenomenology of the social world.* Evanston, IL: Northwestern University Press.

Sigman, S. J. (1991). Handling the discontinuous aspects of continuous social relationships: Toward research on the persistence of social forms. *Communication Theory, 1,* 106-127.

Sillars, A. L., & Scott, M. D. (1983). Interpersonal perception between intimates: An integrative review. *Human Communication Research, 10,* 153-176.

Silver, A. (1989). Friendship and trust as moral ideals: An historical approach. *European Journal of Sociology, 30,* 274-297.

Simpson, J. A. (1990). Influence of attachment styles on romantic relationships. *Journal of Personality and Social Psychology, 59,* 971-980.

Smith, A. J. (1957). Similarity of values and its relation to acceptance and the projection of similarity. *Journal of Psychology, 43,* 251-260.

Smith, N. V. (Ed.). (1982). *Mutual knowledge.* London: Academic Press.

Smollar, J., & Youniss, J. (1989). Transformations in adolescents' perceptions of parents. *International Journal of Behavioral Development, 12,* 71-84.

Sorensen, T., & Snow, B. (1991). How children tell: The process of disclosure of child sexual abuse. *Journal of the Child Welfare League of America, 70,* 3-15.

Spencer, T. (1991, June). *To come out or not to come out: A test of self-disclosure theories applied to adolescent-parent relationships.* Paper presented at the Third International Network Conference on Personal Relationships, Normal, IL.

Spencer, T. (1992). *Self-disclosure in family conversational interaction: Communication between parents and adolescents.* Doctoral dissertation, University of Texas at Austin.

Spencer, T. (1993a, February). *A new approach to assessing self-disclosure.* Paper presented at the annual meeting of the Western States Communication Association, Albuquerque, NM.

Spencer, T. (1993b, June). *The use of a Turning Point Conversation Task to stimulate nearly natural conversation.* Paper presented at the Fourth International Network Conference on Personal Relationships, Milwaukee, WI.

Spencer, T. (1993c, November). *Testing the self-disclosure reciprocity hypothesis within the context of conversational sequences in family interaction.* Paper presented at the annual meeting of the Speech Communication Association, Miami, FL.

Spilich, G. J., Vesonder, G. T., Chiesi, H. L., & Voss, J. F. (1979). Text processing of domain-related information for individuals with high and low domain knowledge. *Journal of Verbal Learning and Verbal Behavior, 18,* 275-290.

Spitzberg, B. H. (1993). The dialectics of (in)competence. *Journal of Social and Personal Relationships, 10,* 137-158.

Stiles, W. B. (1992). *Describing talk: A taxonomy of verbal response modes.* Newbury Park, CA: Sage.

Street, R. L. (1982). Evaluation of noncontent speech accommodation. *Language and Communication, 2,* 13-31.

Strickland, L. H. (1958). Surveillance and trust. *Journal of Personality, 26,* 200-215.

Summit, R. C. (1983). The child sexual abuse accommodation syndrome. *Child Abuse & Neglect, 7,* 177-193.

Sunnafrank, M. (1983). Attitude similarity and interpersonal attraction in communication processes: In pursuit of an ephemeral influence. *Communication Monographs, 50,* 273-284.

Sunnafrank, M. (1984). A communication-based perspective on attitude similarity and interpersonal attraction in early acquaintance. *Communication Monographs, 51,* 372-380.

Sunnafrank, M. (1986). Communicative influences on perceived similarity and attraction: An expansion of the interpersonal goals perspective. *Western Journal of Speech Communication, 50,* 158-170.

Sunnafrank, M. (1991). Interpersonal attraction and attitude similarity: A communication based assessment. In J. A. Anderson (Ed.), *Communication yearbook 14* (pp. 451-483). Newbury Park, CA: Sage.

Sunnafrank, M. (1992). On debunking the attitude similarity myth. *Communication Monographs, 59,* 164-179.

Sunnafrank, M., & Miller, G. R. (1981). The role of initial conversation in determining attraction to similar and dissimilar strangers. *Human Communication Research, 8,* 16-25.

Swinth, R. L. (1967). The establishment of the trust relationship. *Journal of Conflict Resolution, 11,* 335-344.

Taylor, S. E., & Brown, J. D. (1988). Illusion and well-being: A social psychological perspective on mental health. *Psychological Bulletin, 103,* 193-210.

Thomas, D. O. (1978). The duty to trust. *Proceedings of the Aristotelian Society, 79,* 89-101.

Thompson, M. (1992). *Should I stay or should I go now: Ambivalence and the dissolution of dating relationships.* Unpublished doctoral dissertation, University of Waterloo, Waterloo.

Tomkins, S. S. (1981). The role of facial response in the experience of emotion: A reply to Tourangeau and Ellsworth. *Journal of Personality and Social Psychology, 40,* 355-357.

Tracy, K. (Ed.). (1991). *Understanding face-to-face interaction: Issues linking goals and discourse.* Hillsdale, NJ: Lawrence Erlbaum.

van Kleeck, A., Maxwell, M., & Gunter, C. (1985). A methodological study of illocutionary coding in adult-child interaction. *Journal of Pragmatics, 9,* 659-681.

Vangelisti, A. L. (1992). Older adolescents' perceptions of communication problems with their parents. *Journal of Adolescent Research, 7,* 382-402.

Vangelisti, A. L. (1994). Family secrets: Forms, functions, and correlates. *Journal of Social and Personal Relationships, 11,* 113-135.

Vangelisti, A. L., Knapp, M. L., & Daly, J. A. (1990). Conversational narcissism. *Communication Monographs, 57,* 251-274.

Walker, M. B., & Trimboli, A. (1989). Communicating affect: The role of verbal and nonverbal content. *Journal of Language and Social Psychology, 8,* 229-248.

Walker, R. N. (1963). Body build and behavior in young children, 2. Body build and parents' ratings. *Child Development, 34,* 1-23.

Warner, R. M., Malloy, D., Schneider, K., Knoth, R., & Wilder, B. (1987). Rhythmic organization of social interaction and observer ratings of positive affect and involvement. *Journal of Nonverbal Behavior, 11,* 57-74.

Wegner, D. M. (1987). Transactive memory: A contemporary analysis of the group mind. In B. Mullen & G. R. Goethals (Eds.), *Theories of group behavior* (pp. 185-208). New York: Springer Verlag.

Wegner, D. M., Giuliano, T., & Hertel, P. T. (1985). Cognitive interdependence in close relationships. In W. Ickes (Ed.), *Compatible and incompatible relationships* (pp. 253-276). New York: Springer Verlag.

Wegner, D. M., Raymond, P., & Erber, R. (1991). Transactive memory in close relationships. *Journal of Personality and Social Psychology, 61,* 923-929.

White, J. M. (1985). Perceived similarity and understanding in married couples. *Journal of Social and Personal Relationships, 2,* 45-57.

Wilkes-Gibbs, D., & Clark, H. H. (1992). Coordinating beliefs in conversation. *Journal of Memory and Language, 31,* 183-194.

Wiseman, J. P. (1986). Friendship: Bonds and binds in a voluntary relationship. *Journal of Social and Personal Relationships, 3,* 191-212.

Wiseman, J. (in press). Enemies. In S. W. Duck & J. T. Wood (Eds.), *Understanding relationship processes: Vol. 5. Relationship challenges.* Thousand Oaks, CA: Sage.

Wood, J. T., Dendy, L. L., Dordek, E., Germany, M., & Varallo, S. M. (in press). Dialectic of difference: A thematic analysis of intimates' meanings for difference. In K. Carter & M. Presnell (Eds.), *Interpretive approaches to interpersonal communication.* New York: State University of New York Press.

Wood, L. A. (1986). Loneliness. In R. Harre (Ed.), *The social construction of emotions* (pp. 184-208). Oxford, UK: Basil Blackwell.

Wright, T. L., & Ingraham, L. J. (1985). The simultaneous study of individual differences and relationship effects in social behavior in groups. *Journal of Personality and Social Psychology, 48,* 1041-1047.

Wright, T. L., & Ingraham, L. J. (1986). Partners and relationships influence self-perceptions of self-disclosures in naturalistic interactions. *Journal of Personality and Social Psychology, 50,* 631-635.

Zuckerman, M., Driver, R. E., & Koestner, R. (1982). Discrepancy as a cue to actual and perceived deception. *Journal of Nonverbal Behavior, 7,* 95-100.

Author Index

Subject Index

Abuse. *See* Child abuse; Sexual abuse; Family violence
Accommodation, 95f
Acquaintances, 8, 10f, 20
Adolescent individuation, 62ff
Adolescents, 62ff, 69, 70
Affect management, 150ff
AIDS, 46, 47, 48, 55
Ambivalence, 97
Appraisal process, 92, 93
Attachment, 89, 90, 100
Attitude dissimilarity, 113, 115, 116, 119, 124, 129, 132
Attitude similarity, 113, 114ff, 119ff, 129

Betrayal, 105, 106, 107
Bogus stranger, 114

Child abuse, 50, 52, 53
Communication. *See* Family communication; Interpersonal communication; Parent-adolescent communication; Quality communication; Relationship communication; Serial construction of meaning
Competence, 45, 119, 128, 133
Comprehension, 145f
Conflict, 95, 98, 99
Control, 143, 147f, 149, 152, 154, 156, 157, 159, 161
Conversation, 6, 7, 8, 10, 14, 58-60, 65, 69, 71, 76

Deception, 127, 128, 133, 156f
Development of relationships, 41f
Dialectics, 42f, 120
Discourse, 59, 60, 61, 65, 69, 70
Distrust, 90, 107
Dominance, 152f
Dyadic intersubjectivity, 23, 63, 64, 127f

Enemies, 23, 24, 26
Equivocation, 120, 121, 127, 133
Expectations, 101, 103, 104, 105
Expertise, 7, 19, 21, 25
Expressiveness, 44
Extension, 124

About the Contributors

Susan D. Boon, Ph.D., is an Assistant Professor in Psychology at the University of Calgary. She received her doctorate from the University of Waterloo in 1992, where she worked closely with John G. Holmes and his research team for several years. Her primary areas of interest have focused on various issues surrounding trust and risk in romantic involvements, viewed from a social-cognitive perspective.

Kathryn Dindia, Ph.D., is an Associate Professor in the Department of Communication at the University of Wisconsin-Milwaukee, where she has taught for 12 years. She received her doctorate in speech communication from the University of Washington in 1981. She has published research on self-disclosure, communication and relationship maintenance, and gender differences in communication. In 1993, she coedited with Dan Canary a special issue of *Journal of Social and Personal Relationships.* She also hosted the 1993 International Network Conference on Personal Relationships at the University of Wisconsin-Milwaukee.

Steve Duck is presently the Daniel and Amy Starch Research Professor at the University of Iowa, Iowa City. He is the founding editor of the *Journal of Social and Personal Relationships,* the editor of *The Handbook of Personal Relationships,* and the editor or author of 25 other books on personal relationships. He also founded the International Network on Personal Relationships, the professional organization for the field, and two series of international conferences on relationships.

Kathy Garvin-Doxas is a graduate student in the Department of Communication, University of Colorado, Boulder. Her interest in mutual knowledge as it is manifested in communication stems from her work on perceptions of communication competence in second-language speakers of English and of French. In her future work she plans to use ethnographic methods to examine organizational rhetoric, particularly as it is manifested in face-to-face interaction.

Allen J. Hart, Ph.D., is an Assistant Professor in the Department of Psychology at the University of Iowa. He received his doctorate in social psychology from Harvard University. His research and teaching interests include nonverbal behavior and communication, the processes of social influence, and psychology and law. He is especially interested in investigating experimental social-psychological phenomena in applied settings.

Maureen P. Keeley is a doctoral candidate in the Department of Communication Studies at the University of Iowa. She received her master's degree in communication from the University of Arizona. Her current research focuses on verbal and nonverbal communication and their role in the maintenance of personal relationships. She also is developing a self-report nonverbal scale for examination of nonverbal behavior in naturally occurring interactions.

Michael Monsour, Ph.D., is currently conducting research and teaching at the University of Colorado, Denver. He received his master's degree in communication from the University of Arkansas, Fayetteville, in 1983, and his doctorate in communication from the University of Illinois, Champaign, in 1988. He has published in the areas of cross-sex friendships, intimacy, interpersonal perception, and second-guessing. His primary research interest lies in the area of how relational partners in general, and cross-sex friends in particular, construct their relationship through various cognitive and interactional strategies.

Sally Planalp is Associate Professor in the Department of Communication, University of Colorado, Boulder. Three general areas have been the focus of her research: face-to-face interaction, social cognition, and close relationships. She has published a number of articles and book chapters on topics such as conversational coherence, relational schemas, cognitive processes in close relationships, relationship development and deterioration, and differences between friends' and acquaintances' conversations. In future work she plans to do research on emotion to get a richer picture of face-to-face interactions in close relationships.

Ted Spencer, Ph.D., writes, lectures, and serves on committees in the Department of Speech Communication at the University of Maryland at College Park. He received his doctorate from The University of Texas at Austin in 1992. He has taught at Eastern Washington University, DePauw University, and Indiana University at Indianapolis. He currently is researching self-disclosure as a conversational behavior, and has a special interest in teaching etiquette as a contrast to traditional interpersonal communication "skills."